D1445828

THE KIMONO MIND

THE KIMONO MIND

BY BERNARD RUDOFSKY

An Informal Guide to Japan and the Japanese

Doubleday & Company, Inc., Garden City, New York, 1965

Book design by the author

To Governor Masanori Kaneko

Contents

Advertisement   11

The Initiation   19

Kimonology   41

Guidemanship   65

Ladies Last   88

A House for the Summer   112

Hedonism for the Destitute   133

On Language   153

An Appetite for Rice   164

Train Travel   203

Taste by Edict   222

Forbidden Directions   263

Acknowledgments

The author's thanks go to Mrs. Anne Freedgood for editing the manuscript; to Mr. D. L. Philippi for helping me to acquire a collection of Japanese pre-Westernization books that furnished most of the illustrations in this book; to the librarians Miss Elizabeth Roth, New York Public Library, and Mr. Philip Yampolski, Columbia University, for their help in obtaining additional illustrations; more particularly, to Miss Nobuko Uenishi for her candor in interpreting to me things Japanese in general.

A note on the illustrations

No pictures adequately reveal Japan and the Japanese. Whether seen through the eyes of a Hokusai or the lens of a Nikon, the image is misleading. Japan cannot be fathomed as matter-of-factly as England, Holland, or Disneyland. Some danger of misrepresentation is ever-present, indeed, unavoidable.

The woodcuts and drawings that accompany the text are primarily meant to convey some of the *aroma* of the Japanese cultural climate, with its baffling inversion of standards and values. To suggest the quality of the original illustrations, the pages were reproduced as they look to the reader, with the print on the adjacent pages showing through the thin Japanese paper.

The classical Japanese landscape is hydraulic rather than heroic: rain-soaked, mist-hooded, bathed by brooks and waterfalls. From a *Guide to Nikko*, 1728.

Advertisement

As late as the middle of the last century, every continent except Europe held its geographical mysteries. The globe was dotted with blank spaces which were either too hot or too cold for comfort, too dangerous or too poor, attracting only the most dedicated explorers or the most desperate adventurers. It was a time when a subcontinent like Alaska could be bought as readily as a city block in mid-Manhattan and for about as much cash. The only unknown country with a tolerable climate, with a fascinating albeit incomprehensible civilization hermetically sealed against contamination from the outer world, was Japan.

The picture the West had formed of her was rather two-dimensional—a country resembling nothing so much as a stage set. Like many a stage set it was exuberant and stylized at once: scenes resplendent with waterfalls, rocks and misshapen pine trees; swirling brooks and rivers; more bridges than houses; and, to confuse the eye, all this was innocent of perspective, without depth, with only some low

A sampling of animals from a seventeenth-century encyclopedia.

clouds or ground fog to indicate distance.

The beasts and people who animated the moist setting were no less irregular. There was an abundance of dragons but not so much as the shadow of a cow; there were tigers, herons, eagles—a veritable ranch of heraldic animals. Even the human figures did not add much reality to the scene. Western eyes accustomed to the somber colors of nineteenth-century clothes found the Japanese theatrical, an impression strengthened by their smallness—about three-quarters life-size, which is the height of Sicilian marionettes. They were neither children nor dwarfs, just very short. What accounted for their peculiar attraction (for everybody who had come face to face with them commented on their charm), was the way they moved—pattering along jerkily, bowing violently, doubling up, as in a mechanical ballet.

The toy box has long since been pried open, the forbidden land surveyed and assessed, a census taken. The rocks and trees and waterfalls are still there, but they look somewhat frayed in the presence of billboards that advertise the very same waterfalls, trees, and rocks. The flying dragons have turned into helicopters, the tigers into Jag-

uars. The people have taken to wearing sweat shirts and plastic raincoats. They are growing taller every year, and for all we know may grow into giants. And yet, the mystery persists. If anything, it has deepened and darkened.

The ancient legends' sharply defined black-and-white contrasts of good and evil have given way to a thousand melancholy shadings of mediocre goodness and badness. Old virtues and vices are now suffused with schizophrenia. Moreover, everything is impermanent. Everyday life is experimental and brisk (at a Japanese pace) and looks even more so against the background of monolithic tradition. The testing ground of humanism Japan has been called, and a country in transition. Indeed, so long she has been in transition—and will probably remain so—that we ought to consider her as being in permanent transition. The narcotic atmosphere of feudalism, of two-edged swords and two-sworded knights, has yielded to a nightmare of up-to-dateness. The country is one big laboratory on a nationwide scale where the elixir of life is being distilled from the latest formulas. Anybody who wants to study Americanization had better go to Japan these days. Although theirs is a spotty, Japanese Americanism, its fra-

13

grance is overpowering. Except for complexion and stature, the Japanese are the most flattering imitation of Americanhood. None of them seems troubled by the dilemma of how to reconcile the historic concept of their superiority with their eagerness to assimilate the attributes of an alien race. Centuries-long seclusion, at a time when other nations were traditionally engaged in trading merchandise and blows, left an indelible mark on their character. There is something spinsterish about the Japanese. Their breathless pursuit of novel sensations does not quite conceal signs of melancholy regret—an unpleasant awareness of having wasted the pink of condition on internal bickerings.

The Western world came lamentably late upon Japan, and the "opening" brought disappointment. The things that tumbled out of the treasure chest were thought to be ordinary, not to say primitive, by Western standards. Early travelers—the Spanish and Dutch traders—who had taken Marco Polo's golden roofs at face value, soon gave up hope for a big loot. If anything, the country was poor—a land of peasants and fishermen. Even the big towns were no more than sprawling villages. If there were rich people, their riches were not apparent. What caught the eye and

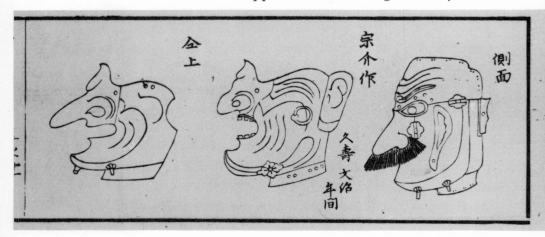

touched the heart was the spectacle of a country at per-
petual peace; a harmoniousness of man and nature that
had departed from the Western world with the advent
of industrialization.

Before the Japanese began to lay waste their country in
the name of Westernization, it must indeed have been paradise. Visitors grew rhapsodic over its charms. "How inviting are the shores with their cheerful dwellings!" exclaimed
Siebold (Japan's Humboldt) when he first entered Nagasaki Bay. "What fruitful hills! What majestic temple
groves!"[1] The picture one gets from these early reports
resembles nothing so much as that of archaic Greece.
In those days when travelers were inclined to quote Homer
rather than the stock market, Japan's shores forever evoked
comparison with classical images. And with good reason.
Japan was in many respects the Oriental counterpart of
Greece, that bucolic-heroic country which Europe had just
then delivered from centuries of slavery under Turkey's
yoke. Like Greece, Japan was blessed with groves of ever
green cedar, oak, and laurel, windswept islands, rocky
beaches, and snowcapped mountains. And towering in the
humid sky was an Oriental Olympus of gods every bit as

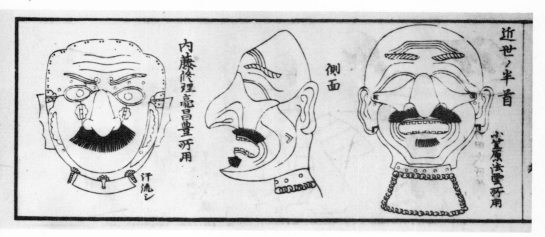

Seventeenth-century masks from a reference book on armor.

eccentric and querulous as that of their Greek cousins.

Commodore Matthew Perry's men were the last to see Japan intact—mostly through binoculars. According to the official *Narrative of the Expedition,* "all the officers and men were in rapture with the beauty of the country; nothing could be more picturesque than the landscapes wherever the eye was directed . . . a scene of beauty, abundance, and happiness, which every one delighted to contemplate."[2] Japan's medieval society, miraculously preserved for two and a half centuries in a nearly perfect state of embalmment, collapsed when the country was forced to join the international brotherhood. The recklessness and speed with which the Japanese caught up with the presumed advances of the outer world made for a great success story. When success went to their heads and led to their downfall, the recovery from disgrace was as spectacular as their erstwhile conversion to Western culture. Her conquerors were thrilled, for nothing appeals to an American more than a redeemed sinner. Our ultimate failure to steer them along the simple lines of joyous redemption is to be blamed, however, less on abstract verbal barriers than on the real gap between two nations harboring absurd opinions about themselves and each other.

For never have two peoples, so utterly different in makeup—excluding a few striking similarities—been so eager to flatter each other, to convert each other, to explain themselves to each other, to study every wrinkle of each other's psyche, to copy, adopt and exchange (after a fashion) each other's proudest achievements—democracy and Zen, beat and Buddhism, striptease and Noh, flower arrangement and baseball—never has there been so much self-examination and cross-examination, so much talk about double alienation and double identification, with so little avail. Japanese have plotted with desperation a path through the muddles of American upper and lower middle-class values, of bureaucratic and academic principles, while Americans have been living doggedly in musty Buddhist convents, inhaling the odor of sanctity and seeking revelation through undernourishment and overfatigue.

Of all the contradictory intelligence we have on foreign peoples, that on the Japanese is the most contradictory. Clichés utterly fail us: Frenchmen are frivolous, Italians are lazy, but what shall we make of the Japanese? They are at once geniuses and copycats, aesthetes and vulgarians; their politeness is as exquisite as their rudeness, their wisdom often indistinguishable from stupidity. Although they carry a heavy burden of comparison with the past, they are nothing less than proud of having transformed a mythical jungle into a modern desert. Many a person who from a distance contracted a passion for Japan and has been fanning it over the years is seized by doubts on approaching Japanese shores. The phantasmagoria of the ultimate sublime may dissolve, he fears, into a mire of mediocrity. Indeed, if he looks for a flash of enlightenment on contact, he is disappointed for even the shores may turn out to be largely metaphorical. What he needs is a divining rod or an article of faith.

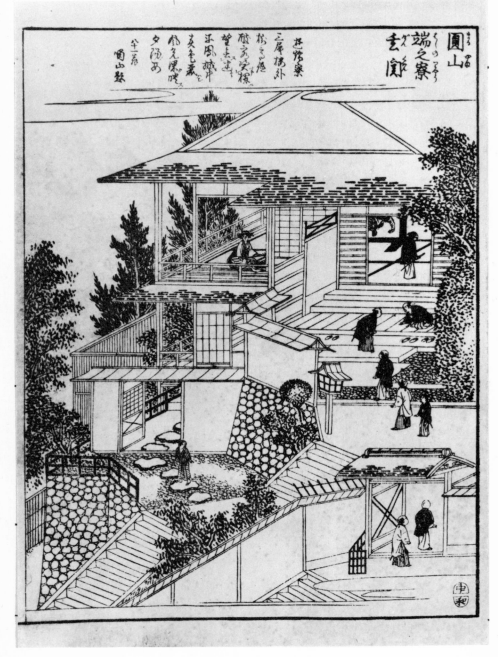

Except for the addition of room telephones, electric lights and electric fans, traditional teahouses and inns have not changed.

The Initiation

Pity the man who cannot muster a feeling of awe, a sort of intellectual creeps, at the thought of visiting Japan. And by visiting I do not mean having a fling with Japan—an all-expense tour with room reservations at the Imperial Hotel. I mean the total immersion in the ooze of a culture as antithetical to ours as it can possibly be. If there are moments of self-doubt, all the better; humility will find its reward. If you "feel indescribably towards Japan," as Lafcadio Hearn put it, if you want to turn your first meeting into a love-match, do not leave a thing to chance. Give it a push in the right direction. The outcome will depend in good measure on your own resources—whether you possess the curiosity and stoicism that mark the true explorer; whether you can summon the abnegation of a novice taking the veil. Make allowance for maxims such as: Time is of no account, or, Language serves for hiding one's thoughts. Be prepared for the fact that in Japan there is no sin, original or otherwise.

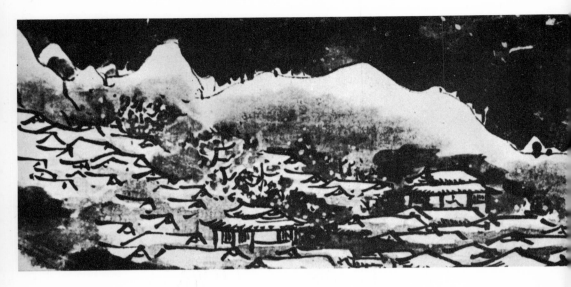

It goes without saying that the right time for a rendezvous with Japan is the first consideration. One trouble with Japan is the fickle weather. Often violent, never intolerable, it is perhaps more than commonly unstable. The Japanese are overly fond of it and celebrate its vicissitudes in that meteorological species of poetry called *haiku*.

"The fan-seller: / A load of wind he carries, / Ah, the heat!" (Kakô).

Or, Sampû: "In the summer rains, / The frogs are swimming / At the very door."

Haiku are short-short poems—to be exact, poems of seventeen syllables; hardly the kind to take your breath away or raise your blood pressure. Their brevity and vagueness recall our whimsical weather forecasts. Alas, the weather does not always live up to either, and moments of poetic flight are eclipsed by long stretches of numbness. Winter is grim, if pretty. Not that it is forbiddingly severe —far from it. It just happens that Japanese houses are unequipped for cold weather. In Japan, hibernation lacks the cosiness that goes with porcelain stoves.

Painting by the poet Yosa-no-Bûson (1716–1783).

"It is cold" and "It is hot" are conventional greetings, not laments. People never complain about the weather. They never think of rainy days as bad-weather days— on the contrary, rain is considered a blessing since it keeps their rice-baskets filled. Typhoons apart, there is no such thing as bad weather, and to farmers even typhoons are more often a benefit than a calamity. Like those other is- landers inured to moisture, the English, the Japanese enjoy rain and fog. The only people who feel unhappy about the rain are foreigners wearing the wrong clothes. Yet, unless one is a poet—there is more than a vein of watery poetry in the Japanese—raindrops falling into a lotus pond do not strike us as different from raindrops falling on asphalt. It is all a matter of upbringing.

Spring, elsewhere the poets' bonanza, in Japan is likely to dampen their spirit. A succession of rainy days, it has little to recommend it to the non-Japanese. Cherry-blossom time, much touted, is but one of the many wet periods that turn the country into one big swamp. There is mud in the fields, mud in the streets, mud in the gardens, and everybody hobbles along on high-stilted rain-weather clogs. Cherry-blossom time, when you get down to it, is a state of mind, a time for merrymaking, for drinking and getting drunk. But the inner warmth generated by hot *sake* provides only moderate immunity against the melancholy side of wetness. Boredom waxes, and the suicide rate climbs to twenty-two per day.

Japan is without doubt at its most becoming in summer. There is rain aplenty, but there are also long days of blue skies. "What happiness, / Crossing the summer river / Sandals in hand!" sings Bûson. During the summer months Japan takes on the radiance of a latter-day Arcadia, with luminous nights, fireflies, and, for good measure, mosquitoes of a mild sting and musical hum. Midsummer, assuredly, is the most propitious time for a visit.

Of far greater moment is the choice of a perfect setting for the first night under a Japanese roof. The circumstances of the first physical contact with Japan, the first embrace so to speak, may spell the difference between affection and dislike. With any luck, the neophyte will experience bedazement, a touch of panic, comparable to the sensation of knowing a woman—in the Biblical sense. The answer to his prayers is an inn.

A true Japanese inn has a utopian flavor; the comfort it offers is unlike anything we know. If its amenities seem to be more in the nature of discomfort, it is only because it is often difficult to draw the borderline between comfort and discomfort as between pain and pleasure of the more exquisite kind. Besides, an inn is not for the mobophile. Anyone attuned to American resort hotels with their kindergarten atmosphere of "planned activities," playgrounds, and tutors, is taken aback by the Japanese taste for seclusion. In Japan, solitude is a status symbol. "The higher the rank, the greater is the seclusion in which the

Print by Suzuki Horonobu (1725–1770).

Three young women indulging in the pleasure of walking barefoot.

individual lives," noted Townsend Harris, America's first consul to Japan.[3]

The rooms and gardens of an inn combine the airiness of a birdcage with the forlornness of a dungeon. The garden —one to a room—is not meant for loafing. Often no more than a few feet deep, it is in the nature of a trompe l'oeil rather than outdoor space. A stuccoed wall or a closely knit bamboo fence screens it off from one's neighbors, barely muffling their voices. There is no restaurant or dining room; meals are taken in one's room. Neither is there a bar at an inn, and even with plenty of corridors, chances of running into another guest are infinitesimal. Moreover, a guest trotting to the convenience place is, according to etiquette, invisible.

A native inn is about as far a point of penetration into Japanese life as Occidentals can hope to reach. But there is the rub: true Japanese inns do not cater to foreigners. Although the rule is broken from time to time, many an innkeeper who weakened has lived to regret it. "After two hundred years of poor success," one of them said, "Japanese innkeepers have given up expecting foreigners to understand their system."[4] For the unwanted there is comfort in knowing that an inn—not just any inn but one of distinction—is not in easy reach of a Japanese either. Money alone does not open its gates. To be admitted, one needs the good services of influential friends. A letter from a governor may be helpful, and again, it may not. Patience is imperative, for the workings of the Oriental mind are roundabout and circumspect. Threatened by inopportuneness of time, a Japanese will choose postponement. A letter going unanswered is not necessarily a snub. Its recipient may be pondering an answer only to find that his thoughts defy translation into words.

Before asking a friend of long standing for what may

24

High garden walls, screens, and tightly woven fences release in the Japanese a delicious sense of entrapment rather than claustrophobia.

The amenities of commercial hospitality are graphically illustrated by Hishikawa Moronobu, 1675.

seem to you a small favor, consider that to grant it may not be in his power. The way to save him from embarrassment is to approach him by a third person. The more vague your request, the better it will be received. Once the ice is broken, however, and acceptance secured, there is cause for jubilation. The honor verges on being admitted to the company of the immortals or being received into the Church.

Withal, the privileges extended seem meager. Although you may come and go as you please, the hospitality is stifling, almost narcotic. Whims and wiles are discouraged. You are not to covet a choice apartment, or maid; you take what you get. The same is true for meals—there is no menu to choose from. You are not allowed to skip a bath or to display antisocial tendencies when sharing bath water with strangers. Moreover, throughout your stay at an inn you are left in the dark about the price of things. When at last you receive your bill, keep in mind that it is not disputed. A bill is for paying. It does not indicate what you are paying for, except in the most summary way: for favors extended. The arrangement has the hallmark of an illicit adventure, and discretion is in order.

The seeming prudishness of the Japanese in money matters, more especially, their reluctance to discuss prices or write out itemized bills, can be traced to their traditional dislike of taking money for what is still considered a personal favor rather than a business deal. In the feudal past, the man who let a wanderer sleep under his roof would no more accept payment from him than we would from a hitchhiker. "The concept of taking money in return for lodgings was vague, if not absent," says historian Kunio Yanagida.[5] Itinerant monks and pilgrims offered prayers instead of money, and nonspiritual travelers paid their way with news and gossip. Noblemen who traveled with a large

27

company were in the habit of taking over an entire house and leaving on their departure a sum of money, correctly gift-wrapped, as a voluntary contribution and token of thanks. A far greater permanent reward was derived from the honor of their visit. In out-of-the-way villages, tourists invariably find their attention directed to some old house that, generations ago, accommodated a traveling *samurai* for a night. From all of which it ought to be apparent that the most heinous crime of a foreigner is to complain of being overcharged. "It is considered ill-mannered," warns Ichiro Kawasaki, "to discuss money matters at an inn, where the innkeeper is supposed to offer his best hospitality regardless of how much will be paid for it."[6]

Pedigreed inns, of which there seem to be lamentably few, are usually tucked away in the shade of ancient castle walls. The castle has disappeared except for some vestiges —moats, gates, a donjon—which exude the moldy aroma of feudalism and thus lend cachet to the inn, a nondescript if elegant structure of uncertain date. Cabdrivers plead ignorance of its existence, and there is no way of knowing whether they are telling the truth or merely conspiring to protect its whereabouts.

For somebody to whom a red carpet and a canopied doorman are essential for a welcome, who thinks of a hotel lobby as a cross between a shopping arcade and a *Kursaal,* the first brush with the pleonastic *nihon-no-ryokan,* a Japanese-style Japanese inn, is a letdown. Often the outside presents a murky picture, and not only does it lack the attributes of commercial hospitality, it does not even pretend to look inviting. Behind a gate set in a garden fence, at the end of a short path half hidden by trees, is an entrance of a sort, paved with cobblestones, suggesting a stable rather than a vestibule. Where the stone floor ends, there is a high step of polished wood and beyond it a

wooden platform. Except for a low screen, the hall is bare
—no reception desk, no pigeonholes for mail, no hooks for
room keys, but then, Japanese doors have no locks. On the
wooden platform are kneeling half a dozen young women,
bowing low and uttering bird-like noises. There are no
pages, no gentlemen in cutaway; in fact, there isn't a man
in sight.

The moment you have wriggled your feet out of your shoes
and stepped onto the platform, there is a tussle—twelve
long-sleeved arms reach out for you and whisk you away in
an onslaught of solicitude and controlled tenderness. The
bevy of maids slither in double step through dark uncar-
peted corridors over polished woodboards that squeak under their white-gloved feet. They do not ask if you want
a snug room or a suite, a room with a view (as a rule,
Japanese rooms don't have views), or if you like to be wak-
ened by the morning sun (every room is tightly shut at
night). At an inner chamber that smells of incense the wild
chase ends as suddenly as it began.

The monkish world of the traditional Japan is closing in
on you—a waft of weariness and dedication. The room is
dark and austere, and while you wonder whether this is
the last word in luxury or whether a door might open to
yet another chamber, one of the maids—the others have
left—begins to undress you. She goes about it briskly, ex-
pertly, silently, like an impatient lover. From a lacquer tray
she fetches a folded gown and mercifully covers your embarrassment. Without a word, she puts her arms around you
to fasten the sash of your gown, a summer kimono of
starched cotton, indigo-dyed, which doubles as nightshirt.
Then, having put away your clothes, she produces cake and
bitter tea. The cake resembles chips of hard green soap, the
sort that hotels provide free of charge with razor blades
and tissue paper. The tea is weak and hot. There is only

one cup—this is not a love feast after all.

Although the Japanese are anything but bashful about body functions, the whereabouts of the Great Convenience Place are not advertised. In some souped-up inns catering to foreigners one comes across signs as "Upsteps please" or "Lady" and "Gentleman," but at an authentic inn with its flavor of mystery, the assistance of an insider is needed to discover what novelist Tanizaki called "the most poetic spot in the Japanese house." The walk through labyrinthine corridors, past hermetic apartments and garden courts, turns into a general orientation course in Japanese hotel architecture. Most privies are located peripherally or whimsically tucked away in secret corners, and, just as a licensed guide is indispensable to the beginner who attempts the ascent of a major mountain, it is the maid's business to show the way. Short of the cunning of a Theseus, one also depends on being escorted back to one's room.

No more congenial setting was ever contrived for the unhurried visitor than the classical Japanese privy: a place for contemplation, a philosopher's den. Its keynote is darkness. Through a small window a weak shaft of light enters, disclosing a curiously appointed cell. The grain of the stuccoed walls is of the finest; the boards of the ceiling are perfectly matched (a sign of impeccable standards); the floor is black lacquer. In lieu of a hollow throne, there is an oblong hole in the floor, lined with porcelain and closed by a wooden cover with a long handle. Porcelain slippers as big as stepping stones flank its sides.

A still life composed of four objects occupies the top of a low cabinet: a single flower, a little drowsy, in one of those rustic jars we have come to identify with Japanese high taste; a tray from which spirals bluish smoke with no more than the suspicion of a scent; an open fan inscribed in terse strokes with a poem, or a thought for the day, or a sample of scatological humor. The fan is not for show but for use. Nowhere on earth does man go about his most humiliating business with so much dignity and abandon.

A teakwood box contains a wad of paper unlike any you ever saw. It is more like a gossamer sheet of snow, if snow could be formed into sheets. It floats in the air like fluff and makes one wish for a skin of peau d'ange. Whatever Japan has in store for you, you know where to find a sanctuary.

The most exquisite privy of them all is never mentioned in English-language books, and this is as good a place as any to remedy the omission. Among the teahouses and sundry buildings that dot the gardens of the Katsura Imperial Villa is a pavilion referred to as the Covered Waiting Bench of the East Side of the Cycad Hill. Guests invited to a ceremonial tea wait here until summoned to the teahouse proper. The modest structure contains a single windowless room, no more than two mats square. Its floor is not matted over, however, but covered in the manner of a dry-garden with earth and several unhewn stones. Tetsuro Yoshida in his *Japanische Architektur*[7] calls it a *Zierpissoir,* an ornamental or mock latrine. It is not and never was intended for the grosser kind of use; it is meant for meditation only.

"The Japanese inn," says *Japan, The Official Guide,* "is an unavoidable necessity unless the greater part of Japan is to remain unexplored," and hopefully adds, "foreign guests will probably be able to turn all seeming inconveniences and discomfort into an interesting experience."[8] After the last war, when Japan was short of hotels, the Ministry of Transportation drafted a number of inns and made them accessible to anyone with cash. No favoritism, no go-betweens. It was as unusual a step as if, say, the Harvard Club merged with Hilton Hotels and was to take

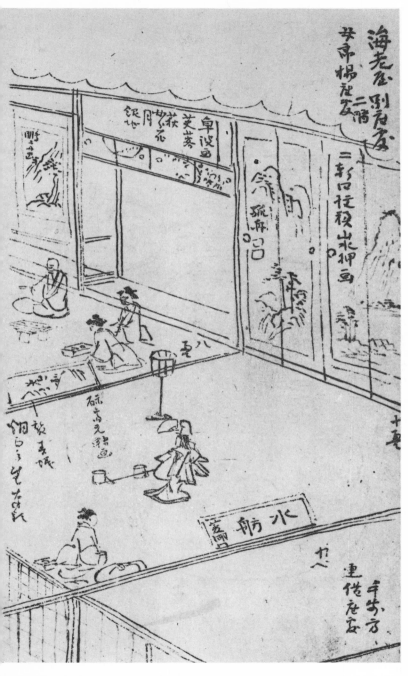

A dinner party in a second-floor apartment of the Ebiya Inn at Beppu. In the foreground two samisen players and, at right, an eight-year-old dancer who appears again in the sketch on page 51. From the notebook of Settan Hasegawa (1778–1843).

directives from the Department of State. Prices were listed for everybody to see; room and board were to be paid in advance with coupons purchased at travel bureaus—a radical departure from time-honored custom.

As early as the turn of the century, when sophisticated globe-trotters began to add Japan to their itinerary, the country boasted a few Western-style hotels—European hotels as they were then called—not much different from those on the China Coast or elsewhere in the Far East. They boldly flaunted their foreignness by advertising incandescent electricity, steam heat and fireplaces, cuisine unsurpassed and Good Old Wines. Native inns were not thought fit to accommodate foreigners and those who did patronize them found much to criticize. "To many," *Terry's Guide to the Japanese Empire* says, "the food is illusive; the fleas inordinately hungry; the toilet arrangements abominable and suggestive of typhoid; the lack of chairs, beds, and other furniture inconvenient; and the native indifference to privacy exasperating. Westerners do not, as a rule, relish the idea of having giggling *nesans,* or serving-maids, traipsing unannounced through their apartments at all hours, whether one be asleep or awake; dressed, undressing or undressed; nor do they want women to scrub them in their baths."[9] Besides, inns were expensive.

Alas, foreigners seldom scale those heights of anthropological detachment that disclose an unencumbered view of an alien culture. They feel that they are missionaries first and guests last. Basil Hall Chamberlain, a man blessed with rare insight and fortitude, took a philosophical view and sided with the innkeepers: "Scanty as the entertainment may often appear to one fresh from the innumerable luxuries of a comfortable European hotel, it should be remembered that such things as fine lacquer and porcelain

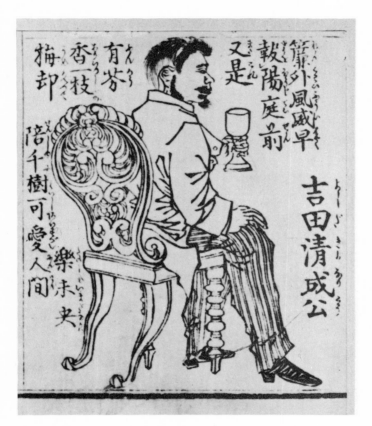

A high-class Japanese who acquired Western polish while studying abroad. From a book of poetry written by heroes of the time, 1879.

utensils, painted screens and silk quilts, to say nothing of numerous well-dressed attendants, are expensive to mine host, and are charged for accordingly."[10] But he did not hesitate to say that the custom of paying *chadai,* tea-money, was vexing.

The gift, always on the generous side, is offered to one's maid *in advance,* not so much to protect her from misers as to avoid even the semblance of a tip. "Don't give small gifts," advises a Japanese gentleman who has closely followed the habits of American visitors, "as if you were buying something the person would rather feel he is offering you of his own free will. The loyalty and performance of Japanese subordinates are taken for granted and not to be bought with cash."[11] To the consternation of foreigners, cabdrivers refuse gratuities, and so do waiters and messengers except in big-city American-style hotels whose managers do their utmost to make their guests feel at home. The maid, having accepted your initial gift, will rush to the nearest shop to buy one for you in turn. (In Japan, gift-giving is performed with methodical madness, and foreigners cast a troubled eye at its unending reverberations of presents received and presents reciprocated. To afford playing the game according to the rules, families have been known to incur debts and go bankrupt. Like a Corsican vendetta, the exchange of gifts comes to an end only with the demise of the adversaries.)

The sweet-tempered *nesan,* the serving maid, is a fixture that has so far withstood the blight of Westernization. *Nesan* means older sister, a euphemism in reverse. If anything, she resembles a younger sister or a nurse, or, rather, a starlet playing a nurse, with a kimono for a uniform. Apart from her duties as chambermaid and personal waitress, she is your constant companion. After she has told you her name—generally of virginal flavor such as "Snow" or "Flower"—so that you correctly address her, she will daunt you with questions about your age, your children, and your profession, in this order. A wife is not a subject for conversation. Her intuition is legendary, her devotion heroic, although both vary slightly with the nature of her charge. The sisterly care she bestows on a single man differs from that for a woman (a woman traveling alone is an anomaly in Japan), while a couple has to be satisfied with her divided attention. She does not know any English.

Perhaps her most demanding task is that of a human thermostat. She alone is responsible for keeping you comfortable through cold and heat. She is a master in fanning; having developed over the years the loose wrist of a violin virtuoso, she is able to maintain a cool jet of air for hours on end. Her other hand is busy mopping her brow since, dressed to the nines as she is, fanning you does not benefit *her*. In winter, when the rooms of an old-fashioned inn turn into man-size deepfreeze compartments, her duty is to tend the braziers.

A Japanese brazier is made of porcelain and looks like an enormous cachepot. It contains from twenty to thirty pounds of ashes topped with live embers which give off some moderate heat but not nearly enough to thaw out your spine. A more efficient if less aesthetic remedy is a hot-water bottle which the maid will stuff between your gown and the several layers of padded outer robes that are worn indoors as a matter of course. Another lifesaver is the glow of charcoals in a fire pit set flush with the floor. When winter winds rattle the house, tearing through fissures and cracks in the bone-dry woodwork, a metal grate and wooden frame are put over the pit and a heavy quilt, thrown over the frame, prevents what warmth there is from escaping too fast. In cold weather, this arrangement also serves as a dinner table. Putting one's feet under the

Sake pot of lacquered wood.

quilt does not encourage blood circulation but saves one from chilblains. It is good form to invite the maid to share the warmth.

She will repay the favor by telling you her autobiography, a heartbreaking story of happy childhood and luckless love, without ever losing sight of the ebbs in your *sake* cup. As you finish drinking the soup from the lacquered bowl—in Japan, clear soup, not dessert, terminates a dinner—she asks: "Shall I bring the bed?"

A man's conduct is largely determined by the taboos and complexes he has acquired in a lifetime and by the condition of the safety valves that control his do's and don'ts. There are no hard-and-fast rules. On this topic, Chamberlain expressed anxiety bordering on dismay: "Too many foreigners, we fear, give not only trouble and offense, but just cause for indignation, by their disregard of propriety, especially in their behavior towards Japanese women, whose engaging manners and naïve ways they misinterpret. The subject is too delicate to be treated here."[12] As indeed it is too delicate to be treated *here*.

The duties of a maid who served you at an inn do not

end with your departure. She rides with you to the railroad station, helps you buy your ticket, checks the baggage ("dangerous articles, portable cooking furnaces, corpses, chicks [sic], will not be handled"),[13] sees to it that you board the right train and get a window seat. This done, she pulls from her kimono sleeve a dainty duster and goes to work on windowsill and windowpane. At last she seems satisfied that nothing is missing for your immediate comfort, and while you nervously listen to bells and whistles, fearful that she might fail to get off the train in time, she settles down in front of you. Apparently she has no intention of leaving.

The train starts moving. You pass in review every hour at the inn, recalling conversations, jokes, teasing words, groping for a cue to your plight. Sensing your anguish she tries to cheer you with a smile, but not until she gets off at the next stop do you breathe again, relieved from the suspicion that somewhere you made a mistake that led to an elopement. Actually it is all a matter of observing the niceties of a polite good-bye.

Mutual attraction between Japanese women and American men is not just a postwar phenomenon. The sailor and kimonoed *femme fatale*—pedestaled, of fashionable silhouette, and in firm control of the bottle—were portrayed by an anonymous artist in the 1860s.

Kimonology

"Do you like kimono?"

The question is popped to the guileless visitor on his arrival, right on the airfield or pier, before he has time to adjust to the frenzied cheerfulness of his hosts. If he answers with misplaced sincerity that he has not had a chance to form an opinion, he will quickly learn his first lesson. The hurt faces—contrary to general belief, the Japanese cannot hide their disappointment—make it unmistakably clear that Japan and the Japanese want to be liked unconditionally.

As a rule the foreigner is delighted to see that the kimono is still around. Emerging from a downtown hotel into his first Japanese morning, he may easily fall prey to the thought that he has been duped by travel folders and travel ads. A Tokyo street, he finds, is no more Oriental than a street in Brooklyn. Perhaps less so. The ugliness of the cityscape comes as a shock to the most cynical sightseer, and so do the disheveled crowds pushing violently and impassively. It takes no time to realize that well-dressed people do not walk in the street. Hence the sight of a kimono is balm for the eye.

Americans seem to be particularly susceptible to the charm of the Old Japan. Cruelly cheated by history of the knights' castles and temple colonnades, they are envious of the relics, genuine or otherwise, that older nations possess in profusion. (The dolled-up men and women who double as ethnical exhibits and museum guards in such neohistorical places as Williamsburg, amount to little more than licensed impostors; rather than representing a link with the past, they add an uncalled-for note of Hallowe'en.)

Costumes and costuming never fail to cast a spell upon imaginative people. To some, the touch of exotic robes is as intoxicating as drugs; to others, strange clothes provide a means of escape from that nearly escape-proof prison, one's self. Still others they help to find themselves. To recapture her lost self-esteem, a woman has been known to buy a new hat. A jewel may bring her blissfulness. But the supreme pleasure afforded by apparel is what I call *sartoriasis,* the enjoyment of discomfort. The kimono fills that need to perfection.

The Japanese author of a book on native manners notes with ill-concealed pride that "the wide sash, or *obi,* worn by Japanese women has been classed with the Western corset and Chinese foot-binding as one of the three great wonders of the world."[14] It is one of those teasing statements that bob like cork on the purling brook of ever-flowing near-misinformation on things Japanese. Are there no other great wonders, one wonders. No pyramids? No hanging gardens? The foreigner has a hard time adjusting to the exclusiveness of the Japanese cosmos. He must learn to cushion himself against cultural shock and to accept gratefully every scrap of intelligence. The quotation

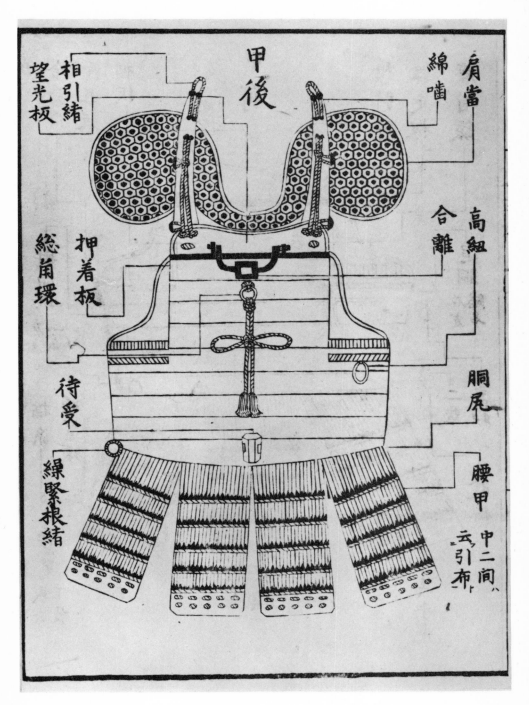

Back side of a suit of armor.

above is a fair example of the sort that comes his way. Disconcerting and candid at once, it puts the finger where it hurts most, or about a handsbreadth above a woman's waist. Elsewhere the same writer points out with equal aloofness that "clothing is said to be the most direct indication of a people's general frame of mind."[15] Putting two and two together, it would seem that the kimono is a legitimate subject for probing the Japanese frame of mind.

The present-day version of the kimono retains hardly any of its former qualities of a loosely flowing garment. On the contrary, ever since the obi, the outer waistband, deteriorated into a rigid affair, it could be counted among the least comfortable types of female dress. As far back as 1887 the empress condemned the wide obi as "unsuited to the human body,"[16] and it would indeed seem a senselessly vicious constriction were it not for the extenuating fact that men derive infinite pleasure from watching hobbled women. They never tire of inventing and perfecting new harnesses for them, putting new obstacles to their gait, all the more as women do not protest against their sartorial captivity. They are happy in their assurance that the bonds imposed on them help to fan a man's desire.

There is more to the kimono than meets the eye. One might say that the outermost wrapper only serves to detract attention from the true nature of the garment—a combination of straitjacket and hobble skirt. Mary R. Beard (*The Force of Women in Japanese History*) observed that the kimono fills a need where too many people live in too tiny dwellings. When they wore the kimono, she says, "tightly about the figure and sat or moved within the smallest compass, domestic life could flow along better thus regulated."[17] A step-by-step account of how to put on a kimono, quoted in abbreviated form from a handbook of the Japanese Tourist Library, discloses a sort of X-ray

A kimono on its rack. The servant girl is no pygmy; her small size merely indicates her low station. Woodcut by Bunnai Tanaka, 1660.

picture of its hidden delights: "First, put on a white cotton vest and silk or cotton underskirt, then the white socks; next, the undergarment is tied at the waist with a waist-tie and an undersash. Then put on the kimono placing the right side under the left. Tie tightly with a waist-tie just below the waist, and draw the extra length of material so that the hem-line will just cover the heels. Fold this down over the tie. Then tie another waist-tie above and wind another undersash around the waist. Next tie the obi."[18] Formerly as narrow as a necktie, the obi has grown into a stiff wide band. The typical discoloration of a Japanese woman's abdomen results from the pressure of the obi.

"Wind the obi," the handbook continues, "around the waist twice. Tie the ends of the obi behind, holding the longer end above the knot and the shorter below. Tug tightly. Fold the longer end down over the obi-bustle wrapped in a bustle-sash and tie the ends of the latter in front, tucking the ends above the obi. Then fold the long end of the obi under, into a tube, tuck the shorter end of the obi into this tube and fasten all these tightly together with the obi-tie. Bring the ends of this obi-tie around in front of the obi and tie tightly there."[19]

Tied in knots, her torso immobilized, her breasts flattened out like flowers between the pages of a herbarium, the Japanese woman now is ready to put into action the deadliest of her secret weapons: her gait. Garment manufacturers' and Broadway producers' opinions to the contrary, a woman's attractiveness is determined less by the degree to which she reveals her body than by the way she walks. Or rather, the way she is restrained from walking. A Japanese lady, noted Townsend Harris, "minces her steps as tho' her legs were tied together at the knees."[20] As indeed they are.

46   In Kyoto, where old customs are observed more fre-

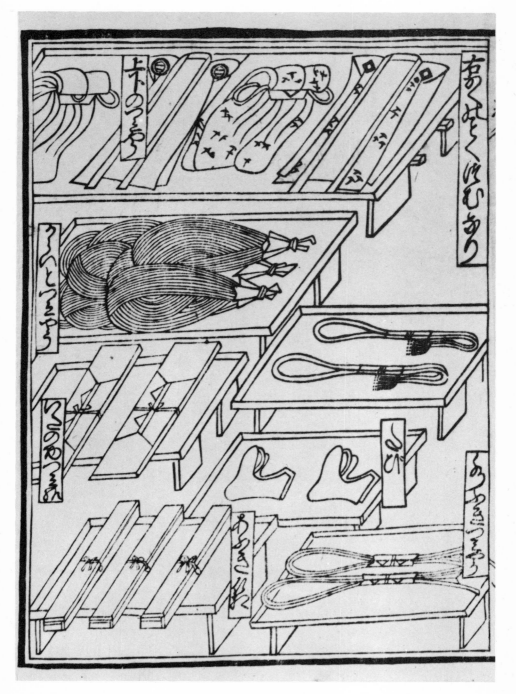

Various components of dress, including cords for tying a woman into a kimono.
From a book of etiquette for women, 1660.

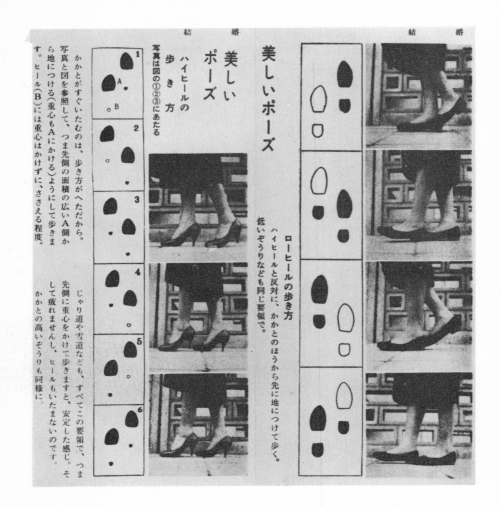

美しいポーズ

ローヒールの歩き方

ハイヒールと反対に、かかとのほうから先に地につけて歩く。低いぞうりなども同じ要領で。

美しいポーズ

ハイヒールの歩き方

写真は図の①②③にあたる

かかとがすぐにたむのは、歩き方がへただから。写真と図を参照して、つま先側の面積の広いA側から地につける（重心もAにかける）ようにして歩きます。ヒール（B）には重心はかけずに、ささえる程度。

じゃり道や雪道なども、すべてこの要領で、つま先側に重心をかけて歩きますと、安定した感じ。して疲れませんし、ヒールもいたまないのです。かかとの高いぞうりも同様に。

A page from a contemporary etiquette book. The diagrams illustrate how to acquire a beautiful *po-zu* (pose) when walking on *hai hiru* (high heels) and *ro hiru* (low heels). Since the correct way to wear Japanese footgear is to drag it, the switch to Western shoes demands practice in lifting one's feet. For some Japanese this is as difficult a feat as learning a new dance step is for us.

quently and more freely than elsewhere in Japan, one still can see a woman's walk performed with pomp. Once a year the queen of the gay quarter is led through the streets in solemn procession. Her sandals are twelve inches high and to keep her balance she depends for support on two women assistants. She moves painfully slowly, dragging the heavy wooden pedestals by her toes only—a grand spectacle of sex appeal compared to which our bathing-beauty contests are kindergarten stuff.

The bizarre custom reflects a taste that is not limited to Japan. Italian engravings of the seventeenth century show Venetian courtesans walking on *chopines* twenty inches high. Like their Japanese colleagues, they are buttressed by two female assistants. Venice at that time was the most Oriental of Western cities (or perhaps it would be more accurate to call her the Westernmost of Oriental cities), and the acrobatics of women towering on stilts were no doubt inspired by the tales of travelers who had seen similar feats performed in the East. The vulgarized form of Venetian walking contraptions, whittled down to a few inches, are today's high-heeled shoes. Like corsets, stockings, face painting and hair dyeing, high heels were pioneered by prominent whores whose leadership in our days has been usurped by the far tougher sisterhood of beauty editors and fashion columnists.

Everyday Japanese footwear is less overt in character than the ceremonial stilts. *Geta,* the wooden soles worn outdoors, resemble furniture rather than footwear. They are rectangular benches, two to four inches high. Sometimes, people actually turn them into benches by sitting on one sole while propping up their feet on its mate, or they may use them as a pillow for the head. *Geta* for adults come in one size only for each sex and are identical for the right and left foot. They have no uppers, no lacings, merely a sort of bridle for the toes. A few hundred years ago they were all-wood contraptions with a knob for the toes to grip, a rakish type still worn by the maids of some archaic inns.

Walking on these veritable footstools is an acquired art, yet walking is not a function that elegant footwear is expected to assist, or even to encourage. Every woman knows that to wear "walking shoes"—as derogatory a term as "sensible shoes"—puts a damper on a man's ardor. The effect of absurdly impractical shoes, on the other hand, is as intoxicating as a love potion. The girl child who puts on a pair of high-heeled shoes is magically propelled into womanhood.

Japanese footwear is at once more sophisticated and more versatile than ours. The pedestals serve a double purpose—to elevate the wearer symbolically and to unbalance her physically. The higher the platform, the thinner the understructure. *Ashida,* the tallest of rainwear *geta,* rest on stilts no more substantial than the bridge of a violin. The sight of a woman unaccountably floating several inches above ground reveals more about Japanese taste than a course in "art appreciation." The wooden stilts also act as percussion instruments and make walking a noisy affair. In some parts of the country, women wear special *geta* for dancing which, on stone pavements, produce a sound indistinguishable from castanets.

The opinions of Westerners on native costume are divided. The early travelers, steeped in the orthodoxy of their own dress, could hardly be expected to rave. The close re-

Four sketches of a famous geisha by Settan Hasegawa. The genuine geisha, an overbred, overripe type of entertainer, not necessarily of great beauty, fails to amuse a non-Japanese. *Geisha-girl* is an American solecism, indiscriminately applied to barmaids and waitresses.

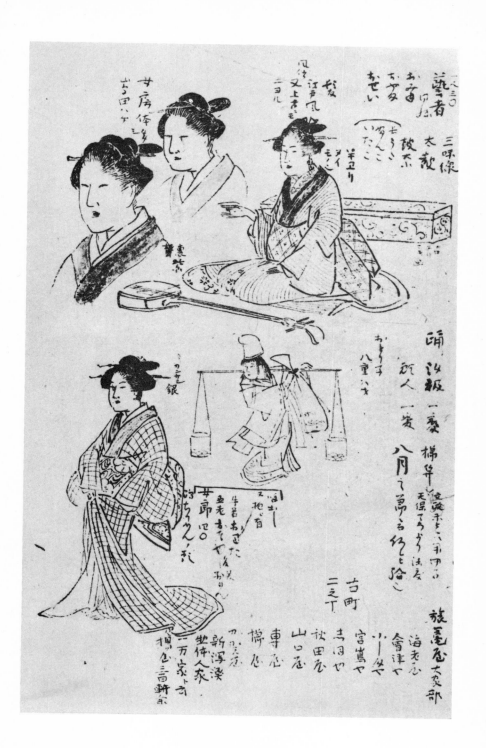

semblance of male and female attire ("The women dress much like the men")[21] was unnatural to people who could not anticipate today's play clothes, so-called. So was the egalitarian character ("Their dress is uniform from the monarch down").[22] The hieratic elegance of Oriental garments had not yet caught the imagination of people to whom leg-of-mutton sleeves and baggy trousers were the height of sophistication. In their eyes, Oriental dress, like ancient Greek dress, was slovenly. Commodore Perry had his disapproval of Japanese women's clothes recorded in his official report—"ungraceful drapery" he called them, "with much of the undress look of nightgowns."[23] For a man to whom an uncorseted woman was no lady, it must have been a shocking sight.

Most Oriental clothes are the antithesis of Western ones. They are cut, if at all, along geometric lines—squares, rec-

To Japanese eyes, Western trousers had all
the elegance of a hollowed-out tree trunk.

When not in use, kimono are folded flat and kept on shelves. Traditional dress fabrics are woven about eleven inches wide and sold by the *tan* (about twelve yards), the amount needed for making one *kimono* (literally, clothing).

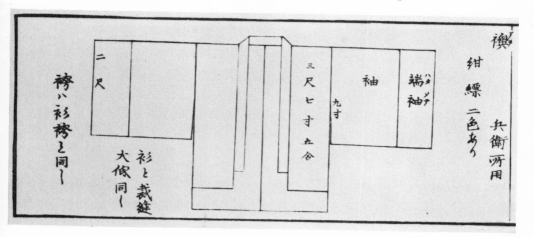

tangles, or circles—which prompts us to call them shapeless. (Today, as in Perry's time, a shape means to most males an hourglass.) Whereas Oriental clothes are innocent of the body's curves, Western clothes are constructed with an eye to anatomy. Intricately shaped, stiffened, and molded, they represent a sort of hollow casting of their owner. Between airings they hang like human effigies from the gallows of our clothes closets. The *modern* kimono belongs to neither of these categories. Spread out flat it is unmistakably Oriental; when it is put on, however, it becomes another kind of garment altogether. It hugs the body as tightly as any tight-fitting dress.

Scanning old prints, one realizes how far Japanese dress has strayed from its more attractive ancient forms. Above all, it has lost the suppleness that enamored generations of woodblock artists. The flowing robes of the past made way for a wrapper as clinging as the tobacco leaves of a cigar with the obi for a cigar band. The bandages cancel out the female form, but then, a woman's breast holds no aesthetic

53

interest for a Japanese man. Neither brassière nor strip-tease, two imports from the West, succeeded in titillating his optic nerve. What does excite him in the way of anatomy is the nape of a woman's neck, particularly when framed by a rear neckline.

A similar transfer of erotic interest from front to rear occurs farther down. What was once a knot tied into a woman's waistband has proliferated into a dorsal hump, compensating no doubt for the lack of a bosom. The knot is not a knot anymore, neither is it a bow, but a cushion wrapped in obi-cloth, a papoose minus baby. A shawl or a short coat, thrown over hump and shoulders, produces the characteristic, now-fashionable hunchback silhouette. The hump looks most un-Oriental; it seems to belong to the protuberances so typical of Western dress—the farthingales, the bustles mimicking steatopygia, the many contraptions for simulating pregnancy.

Gone, too, is the coeducational look. For centuries Japanese gentlemen and ladies dressed so much alike that to tell one from the other in the old prints is often difficult. Japan has a long-standing tradition of transvestism. The court nobles of the so-called military epoch "deemed themselves best attired when they resembled women most closely, shaved their eyebrows, painted their cheeks and blackened their teeth . . ."[24] Not until the nineteenth century did Japanese men begin to feel self-conscious about their attire. "A sight indeed it must have been!" reminisced Fukuzawa,[25] one of the first Japanese to appear abroad in his native outfit. To the trousered and booted Westerners, the swishing skirts, the patter of sandals, suggested women. "You look up and are disappointed," sighed the Russian Ivan Goncharov.[26] The only bisexual garment of today is the *yukata,* an unlined cotton wrap worn to the bath. Formerly never seen outside the house, it has become the

A fashion plate of 1773, showing the bosomy *back* part of traditional dress. *Geta* were angular, and it was good form not to wear foot socks.

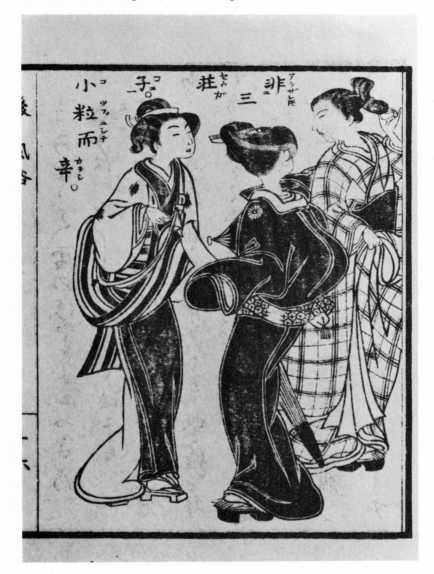

all-purpose dress for visitors to watering places. Regardless of the sex of its wearer, it overlaps to the right.

The decline of the traditional costume has been speeded up by many incongruous additions. Sometimes it is just a touch of foreignness that messes up its pedigree, such as the

"Two under one umbrella," color woodcut by Ishikawa Toyonobu (1711–1785). Clues to their sexes are his sword and her hair ornaments. For another example of legitimate transvestism, see page 107.

glossy *wedge*-soled slippers that have come into favor with kimono-clad women. Japanese feet are broad and short, and these qualities were traditionally emphasized by square, *horizontal* soles which like the pedestal of a statue left plenty of space around the foot. Today's woman fancies soles several sizes smaller than her feet, so that by contrast her feet appear bigger than they are.

The paper umbrellas of old have long been replaced by our bat-like cloth umbrellas, but the most anachronistic note of a contemporary kimono outfit is the handbag of leather or shiny plastic introduced, we are told, by foreign moving-pictures. In the past, small objects were carried in the sleeves of the kimono or tucked under the obi. Today, the only extra function of kimono sleeves is their use as handkerchief—not for wiping her nose but for mopping up the flood of tears a woman is bound to shed at the theater. The Japanese man has transferred the contents of *his* sleeves to a briefcase, and although it may contain nothing more confidential than a box lunch of boiled rice, it is regarded as a status symbol.

Where the fashionable woman truly goes to pieces is right on top: her hairdo is the acme of disorientalization. The permanent wave has eroded the Japanese woman's racial conscience to a degree where any and all scruples about her mongrel costume cease to exist. Whereas in the old days to have curly hair was a fate worse than death, today even a peasant woman cannot do without it. Disowning her luxuriant straight hair, she has reached a point of no return in the pursuit of Westernization.

If older generations had misgivings about Western clothes, it was not because they thought them ugly, but because they were foreign. And foreign they have remained. Even at the height of summer, a Japanese man wears long underwear in order to keep his street clothes from touching

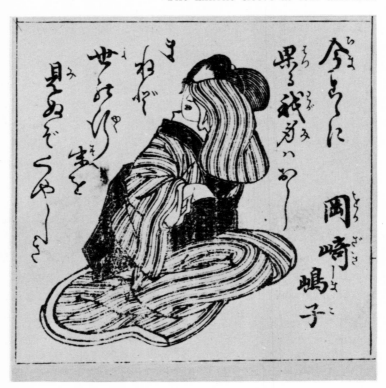

his body. At every opportunity he will take them off and foreign women tourists look with mixed emotions at Japanese men who, having boarded a train, begin to unbutton their trousers and strip to the unmentionables—in their eyes the only unobjectionable garment of Western civilization. Yet, although trouser crease and laced shoes are incompatible with their custom of sitting on the floor, it has never occurred to them to devise an improved version of Western dress to go with their un-Western habits. They take Western clothes as much for granted as brewing ceremonial tea with chlorinated water.

A certain amount of confusion is unavoidable. Especially to the peasant, the distinction between male and female Western attire is either not always clear or he feels free to ignore our sillier conventions. If it suits him, he may wear a veil with his straw hat or bobby pins in his hair. The old man traveling in a Swiss-embroidered shirt is not a transvestite; the girl clad in a nightshirt, driving a motorcycle, is not a strumpet—both chose the garments for their airiness. Paradoxically, shoes, the curse of Western dress, seem unobjectionable to them. Ladies' slippers are looked at as a godsend by Japanese men who are short and have tiny feet. They don't go in for spike heels but find a little wedge or an open toe quite attractive.

When felt hats, leather boots, and tubular dress were decreed by law, and an imperial edict informed the nation that European clothes were concomitants of a more civilized life, the Japanese found a compromise in retaining the native costume for intramural use and as holiday dress. Their genius for avoiding clear-cut solutions enables them to assimilate things foreign without budging in their old ways. Not for them the anguish of having to make a choice, not for them the scruples of the convert. How inconsequential, one muses, was their sartorial revolution compared to the one that took place fifty years later at the other end of the Asian continent, when some of Kemal Pasha's Turks preferred to hang rather than part with their fez. As so often in their history the Japanese were able to have their cake and eat it too. Compromise, however, carries its own penalty. If the Japanese took to Western clothes without enthusiasm or sympathy, Western clothes took to the Japanese even less kindly.

A Western woman in kimono may be a frightful sight, but so are quite a few Japanese in Western clothes. It is all a matter of style. Japanese deportment, rather than losing its flavor in Western-style clothes, acquires a pungency all of its own. A Japanese woman in Western dress who walks in her accustomed way with toes turned in, strikes one as being afflicted with a physical defect. Her walk is a kimono-conditioned posture; without kimono it looks odd. Her elaborate motions of opening and closing a sliding door—she has to kneel down because the door moves only when grasped a few inches above the floor—seem in perfect harmony with her native costume. These genuflections, however, look absurd when she does them in a short skirt and stocking feet. Men, by the way, don't come off any better. Prostrate in formal greeting, they radiate great dignity when clad in traditional robes. The same men performing the same salutations in shirt sleeves look like so many daddies playing horsie.

There is little doubt that the Japanese rate their native clothes second to none. Anyone boarding a Japan Air Lines plane in a U.S. port can sense the precarious balance of East and West at a distance of several thousand miles from the land of the rising sun. A first-class ticket buys service and solace from a kimono-clad stewardess, while the tourist-class tourist has to put up with attendants in Western-style clothes. Without recourse to a single word, the unsubtle message conveys the superiority of Japanese things over Western ones.

On the other hand, a Japanese will concede without prodding that Western clothes are "practical," which means to him that, like everything Western, they need no upkeep. Ask for a clothes brush, and he will produce a singular collection of tools but nothing resembling a clothes brush. It turns out that traditional dress does not need brushing. A kimono is washed. The procedure is tedious beyond description; the garment has to be taken apart and, after washing, resewn. Withal, their methods of washing are lamentable. Some of the most distinguished visitors to Japan, men celebrated for their wisdom and poise, have been seen to burst into tears at the

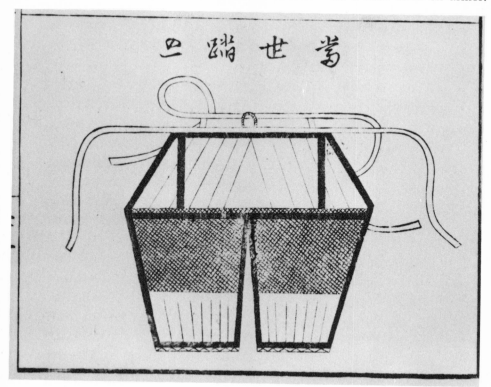

當世踏巴

sight of their shirts back from the local laundry, and any-one who has had a chance to observe a Japanese mistreat-ing a hat or a perfectly good suit of clothes cannot help being struck by his hostility. Japanese contempt for West-ern dress is perhaps most transparent in their treatment of shoes.

In Japan, leather shoes are constitutionally unclean, a hangover from the time when handling leather was the business of outcasts. Even a factory-new pair is tainted, much as an unchristened baby is tainted by Original Sin. Country roads and city streets being forever dusty or muddy or both, shoes become encrusted with the soil of the land. Like the galvanized baby shoes on father's desk, they are transformed, as it were, into some other physical matter

61

Unlike modern ankle-high *tabi,* earlier models reached to the calf.

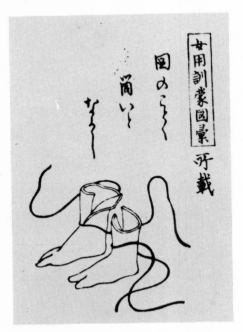

while retaining the shape of their former state.

Whatever their appearance, shoes are not subjected to cleaning—not even at an inn—an omission that hastens their doom since an occasional street shoeshine (always administered by a woman) hardly amounts to an attempt at resuscitation. Being inadmissible to a Japanese house, they are either left outdoors or quarantined in the shoe closet of the entrance hall. In winter, the shoe box turns into a veritable icebox; trying to get into a pair of deepfrozen boots feels like being put to some Oriental torture.

A Japanese man fastidiously avoids touching his shoes with his hands. When he leaves a house, they await him at the doorstep on a well-sprinkled stone floor, sometimes in a puddle of water. A shoehorn, almost as long as a sword, saves him from stooping. (For emergencies he always carries a pocket shoehorn.) Partly because Japanese shoes are of poor quality, partly in consequence of their ill-treatment, they fade away prematurely. Allergic to the water cure, uppers rot, soles curl and die. Still, since pinching shoes are the symbol of progress, the Japanese wear them with confidence.

No sumptuary laws or imperial edicts have been passed in recent years, and people have learned to take their dual wardrobe pretty much for granted. Sartorial promiscuity and sartorial anachronisms cause them no qualms. On the surface the marriage of the old and new is a supremely happy one. The life of a Japanese who daily shuttles back and forth between the existence of an office clerk and that of a greatly reduced *samurai* is apparently much less unhealthy than anthropologists and psychologists will have it. His union suit sticks out from his kimono at neck, wrists, and ankles like an imperfect chrysalis, but this does not affect his serenity. Indeed, it is doubtful whether he is aware of it.

Painting by the poet-painter Uragami Gyokudo (1725–1820).

Guidemanship

Of all the ancient arts prized and practiced by gentlemen, none has been more subject to change than traveling. Tourism made a clean sweep of it and reduced it to a sort of itinerant euphoria. The traveler is made to stick to a schedule, and great care is taken that he never wants but also never lingers nor strays. This applies particularly to Japan. According to the Japanese Tourist Industry Office, twenty-three days are sufficient for an "extended tour."[27] To discourage leisurely travel the Japanese government limits tourist visas to sixty days. If the visitor cannot take a hint and insists on petitioning the authorities for a month's grace, he is in for a lot of red tape.

Whatever else modern communications have done to travel, they have taken the edge off its happier moments. The element of surprise, the exhilaration that comes from personal discovery are largely missing. What has taken their place is pure and simple recognition, and even that may fall behind one's modest expectations. That powerful medium of communication, photography, has succeeded in creating illusions of perfection which reality rarely lives up to. The serenity that emanates from the photograph of a Japanese cryptomeria grove is difficult to recapture by looking at the real thing, surrounded by thousands of sightseers in a far from contemplative mood. Most of them started out in tightly organized units which now have come apart, bogged down in a stalemate. Group captains are rallying their forces, waving pennants, shouting orders, only to have their voices drowned in the bedlam of loudspeakers whose plastic trumpets are nestling obscenely under the eaves of the trees. Several more busloads of pilgrims entering the scene in assault formation, break up and form human pyramids to have their picture taken. In the shade of the trees, dozens of tiny tots are absorbed in painting near-identical pictures of the holy place. Picnics are in progress, litter runs high.

Sometimes the very familiarity of the photographic image is liable to spoil what little remains of the pleasure of exploring. A case in point is Katsura Palace, the imperial summer villa near Kyoto. Ever since its belated promotion to an architectural monument par excellence, it has been described, discussed, and depicted so exhaustively that, when confronted with it at last, one feels one could walk blindfolded through its buildings and gardens. They have, as it were, a quality of déjà vu. Only rarely does one still get ensnared in a discovery of a mild and inconsequential sort, as I myself did several years ago. For one fleeting moment it held the promise of adventure, even though cause and challenge could be traced to nothing more portentous than the reading of a handbook.

Japan, The Official Guide is not the kind of book one would care to read in bed, nor is it likely to arouse one's desire to visit Japan. It treats the subject in a drab, not to say bored, way, and although it lists the addresses of every Tax Administration Office and District Court, it never mentions, say, the existence, past or present, of Yoshiwara or Shimabara. What nevertheless made me read it from cover to cover was immoderate curiosity and some vague hope of coming across some rare piece of intelligence. On page 815 of the Revised Edition, 1954, my perseverance was rewarded; in fact, what I found surpassed my expectations. What caught my eye, almost stopped my breath, was a short note on Naruto, a harbor town on the east coast of Shikoku, known for the spectacular whirlpools in the nearby channel that connects the Pacific Ocean with the Inland Sea. The note in question, however, referred not to its scenic attractions but to an annual event, a kite-flying festival established more than two hundred years ago. "The festival," it said, "is held on every windy day in July and August. More than 1000 kites are flown, some as large as 53 ft. in diameter and 8800 pounds in weight. It requires 200 people to fly each of these giant kites." This is Japan, I told myself with awe and perhaps a twinge of incredulity.

I had never heard of kites weighing as much as two big automobiles and was unable to imagine what they would be like. Four-ton kites seemed every bit as unreal as the wings of Icarus. Whichever way one looked at them, the figures were startling, not to say fantastic, and for one distressing moment I thought I had fallen a victim to a typographical error. On second thought, it appeared unlikely that three misprints would occur in one short sentence. No, I assured myself, here was authoritative information compiled by scholarly experts whose assistance the Ministry of Transportation had acknowledged with deep gratitude. Naruto alone seemed worth a trip to Japan.

Jealous of my discovery and secretly hoping that other readers of the *Guide* would never reach page 815, I began to consult encyclopedias, guidebooks, superannuated and modern. None mentioned the giant kites. Letters to the local authorities remained unanswered or brought ambiguous replies. I learned only what I had already known: although quite a number of Japanese towns observe kiteflying festivals, Naruto is not among them.

Was I to take the *Official Guide,* my only source of information on the Naruto kites, at face value? The flight schedule—every windy day in July and August—seemed excessive. How many windy days, I wondered, has Naruto's windy season?. Moreover, what kind of Japanese were those people who could afford to spend the better part of summer at play?

Having flown all sorts of kites in my childhood, I am familiar with their temperamental behavior. To be sure, my experience had been limited to rickety contraptions weighing no more than a few ounces, or pounds at best. It left me without a clue on how to lift a four-ton kite into the air, or how to land it without smashing it to bits. Were the giant kites of recent design or were they relics of Old Japan? Were they collapsible? Were they stored in hangars or built new every year, and what were they made of— wood? bamboo? silk? paper? One particular question haunted me: did people ever take to the air in them? Probably yes. A skinny fellow, I figured, is negligible ballast for a kite a hundred times his weight. Would the Narutons let *me* make an ascension by kite? If so, would a parachute provide for my safety? I felt I was on the verge of a minor discovery. The stupendous toys cast a new light on Japan, the air fairly crackled with expectation.

Matters did not progress when I reached Japan. The more I labored to enlarge my poor knowledge about the flying monsters, the more they receded into unreality. Casual inquiries led nowhere. No one seemed to have as much as heard of fifty-three-foot kites. Even more distressing, no one seemed to care. I also noticed that some people were offended by my antiquarian interests. Having heard and read about their touchiness, I was not altogether unprepared for their reactions. "Whatever you do," Chamberlain had warned as long as three generations ago, "don't expatiate in the presence of Japanese of the new school on those old, quaint and beautiful things Japanese which rouse your most genuine admiration; speaking generally, the educated Japanese have done with their past."[28] Evidently my curiosity seemed pointless to the educated Japanese; what *they* wanted to talk about was the brave *new* Japan—airplanes, motorships, electric trains. At times it looked to me as if all Japanese had entered a conspiracy against kite-flying. Had I touched upon a sore point—were the kites of Naruto sacred toys? Or secret weapons? The thought crossed my mind that all the jocular references to the mysterious East were essentially symptoms of ill-concealed frustration at our failure to penetrate the veil of Oriental reticence. The only course left to me was to go and look for myself.

On a bright August morning I set out for Tokushima City, the prefectural capital, which is only a few miles distant from Naruto. It was as windy a day as one could wish for flying kites, yet none were visible in the blue sky. No kite-flying contests had been announced or even conjectured. The event that took me to Tokushima was the three days' *Awa Odori,* a dance festival as noisy and frenzied, I had been told, as Rio's Carnival. It was the first day of celebration, and there could be no doubt about its popularity. All highways and country roads leading to the capital were clogged with cars, buses, trucks, three-wheelers, motorcyles and bicycles carrying men, women, and children, many in dance costumes. The road I traveled led

69

through a landscape that Chamberlain, that foremost connoisseur of Japan, had rated as "one of the quaintest and most original" that the country has to offer.[29] The entire classical landscape repertory was present—fanciful volcanic cones and table-mountains, lakes and thousand islands and, as pièce de résistance, a mountain pass right out of the old romances. At times, progress was painfully slow, and although the distance I traveled was barely sixty miles, one day seemed not long enough.

Like most Japan-based anecdotes, this one, too, is rather pointless: only after nightfall did I reach my destination, a sprawling, faceless town, in no way different from hundreds of others. The last stretch had to be done on foot. The streets leading to the center of the town formed one continuous dance floor, with serpentines of dancers, musi-

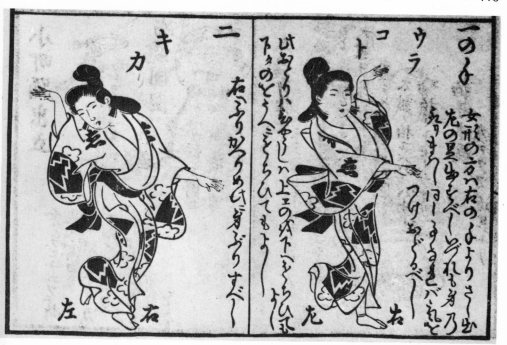

cians, and singers winding their way through the crowds, the women making a deafening racket with their dancing *geta,* and for the next hour I withdrew into a deep and pleasant stupor. I was jolted out of it at a midnight dinner when the governor of Tokushima Province told me that the last of the giant kites of Naruto had been flown in 1914.

Almost all information, official or otherwise, that is offered to the traveler in Japan turns out to be inexact. In spite of a network of travel organizations, of eye-filling posters and pamphlets, of bold concessions to the tastes of the new tourists; in spite of good will (of a highly obstinate sort), the foreign visitor has a hard time making his way through the country. Moreover, cooperation may be withheld if he does not submit to a well-tried routine. Travelers with an independent mind, who rely on their own knowledge and educated hunches rather than on native advice, are considered a nuisance. In the eyes of the Japanese, the foreigner is a babe in the woods, a mixed-up creature, irresponsible and, alas, irritable. Only watchfulness and firm guidance can save him from disaster.

The care and control of foreign travelers is carried out according to peculiar doctrines. A visiting celebrity presents no difficulty; whoever turns out to be a so-called number-one man—it matters little whether he is the greatest living surgeon or the greatest matchbox collector—is accorded a full measure of attention. Chiefly to prevent his straying from the right path, he is assigned a bodyguard

Water parties on the Kano River near Kyoto. Box lunches and singing girls are provided by restaurants but the chief attractions are coolness and the sound of the flowing water.

of devoted men and women who put as much effort into protecting him from what are considered unwholesome aspects of the country as in opening for him doors that lead to legendary treasures and pleasures. He is made a prisoner of Japanese hospitality, and few have been known to evade their polite captors successfully. All they want of him in return are his pronouncements of Japan. He is drawn out about his impressions (however erroneous) on any number of subjects: sights, sounds, tastes, and smells of things Japanese; their perfection, their beauty, above all, their uniqueness. Touched by the passionate interest his hosts take in his every utterance, the honored guest would have to be a lout to withhold applause. Barring some un-

fortunate experience, he ends up with a chronic case of Japanophilia.

Less distinguished travelers who do not rate honorary attendants are urged to engage the services of a professional guide. "In the large cities like Tokyo, Kyoto and Osaka," the *Official Guide* suggests, "time and money, in the long run, are saved by employing a guide." Depending on just how far one intends to venture from the well-marked trail, a guide, to believe the *Guide,* is "important," "invaluable" or "almost indispensable."[30] Nothing could be further from the truth.

A Japanese guide, be he professional or amateur, bears only a small resemblance to guides elsewhere. He brings to his job a steely kind of idealism, with a touch of lunacy. He does not so much indulge in his own idiosyncrasies as in national prejudices. The discrimination he wields is not based on any philosophy but echoes the general belief about what foreigners ought to see in Japan and what they must *not* see. Consequently if you tell him you want to visit the local museum, he may choose to take you to the zoo. Ask him to take you to the zoo, and he will show you a temple instead. He will never tell you his reasons for doing so and will meet your remonstrations calmly. (Irate words are of no avail since they make you lose face; the pleasurable release of anger is unknown in Japan.) Dismiss him and you merely land in the hands of another, equally headstrong fellow. It so happens that a Japanese guide is not a guide in the accepted sense but a sort of ambulant baby-sitter whose principal task is to keep his charge out of mischief but who does not feel obliged to humor him.

The best approach to the Japanese mentality, it has been said, is not to expect the expectable. Because a Japanese attaches little importance to the inveterate habit of ours called thinking, his reactions are often the very opposite of ours. By relying on a stock of ready answers to ques-

No Elsinores, Japanese castles are as neat and almost as inflammable as teahouses; one takes one's shoes off for climbing a donjon. Sketch of Himeji Castle by Nanko Haruki, 1788.

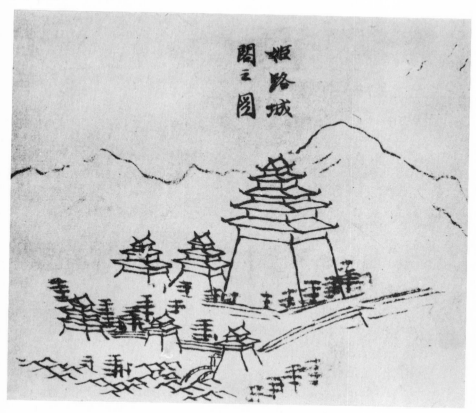

tions, and ready-made solutions to conflicts, he manages to dispense with thinking altogether. A streetcar conductor, says D. G. Haring in *Comments on Japanese Character,* carries a book of rules containing "all possible questions that passengers might ask, together with correct replies. His speech is confined to these prescribed sentences."[31] To put it another way, he knows the answer before he even hears the question.

The Japanese have always considered thinking unreliable, lucidity vulgar, and they are traditionally hostile towards that most impudent of brain exercises, logical thinking. In Japan, truths are discovered, the *Encyclopedia Americana* notes, "by a kind of mental seizure which depends upon the working of a lively and picturesque imagination suggesting to the curious intellect an answer to its problem." Logic being unobtainable for them, they despise it. They seldom miss an opportunity to point out its pitfalls.

Japanese nonlogic in its crudest form turns up in a systematic sabotage of one's wishes. Guides merely set the pattern of the national willfulness. The tourist who orders fish in a restaurant will be served meat. A room reservation for a native inn will land him in a Western-style hotel. A Japanese fondly believes that he may disregard the words of a foreigner for he *knows* that foreigners prefer meat to fish, a Western room to a Japanese room. (This does not apply to the new crop of city hotels and restaurants expressly designed for the needs of the most unbending foreign tourist. These places are indistinguishable from those other vending machines of travel comfort, American chain hotels.)

The foreigner who is not lightly put out, who wants to get to the bottom of things Japanese, ends up as a walking questionnaire. Excited by unfamiliar sights, confronted by unfamiliar situations, he is prone to ask questions by the hour, unaware that a Japanese finds this not only embarrassing but outright rude. Our way of asking questions rattles him. Any answer he might want to formulate is blocked by a mélange of hesitation and false modesty that is all but indistinguishable from arrogance. To evade an answer he will pass the question on to another person—anybody in sight: chauffeur, waitress, or servant. "If a person is asked in a group what his name is," observed the social anthropologist John F. Embree, "he will smile and perhaps ask somebody else to tell it."[32] The directness of our queries, indeed, the very nakedness of our speech, makes a Japanese squirm. To his mind, straight questions and straight answers have the awfulness of an unnatural act.

The mind of a Japanese runs on a different track, and when signals get mixed up as they invariably do, it comes to a halt on a siding. What makes it stall is not necessarily an inability to grasp the question. It simply happens that there is no corresponding answer in his memory or book. Taught from childhood to observe do's and don'ts whose

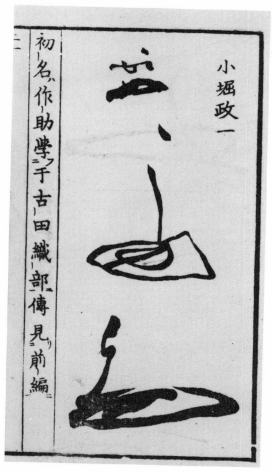

The signatures of some Japanese are not just illegible but mystifying. The cobra-like scrawls spell the name of the tea-master Masaichi Kobori. From an *Index of Signatures,* early nineteenth century.

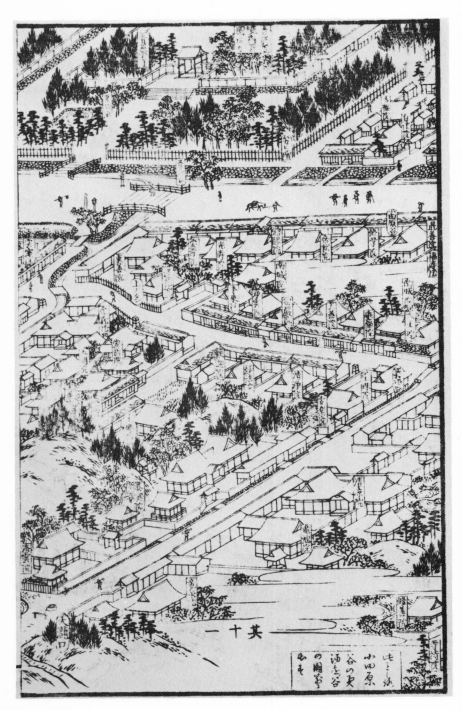

Now rarely visited by foreigners, at the turn of the century the mountain monastery Koyasan near Osaka was counted among the foremost attractions of a trip to the Orient. Repeatedly ravaged by fire, it still boasts 120 temples.

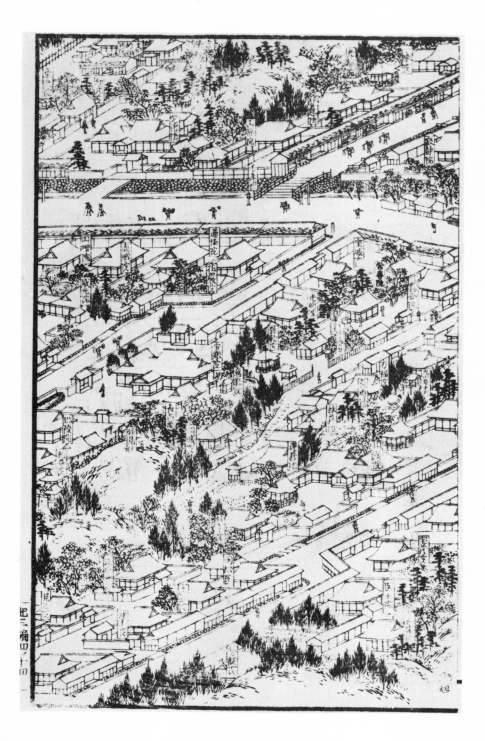

intricacies might drive any but a Japanese out of his mind, he derives from their observance a self-assurance that we cannot hope to achieve by reasoning.

This stolidness is more than made up for by his hospitality, or rather, his arbitrary, not to say despotic, manner of welcoming, entertaining, and sending off his guests. This hospitality is anything but a myth—it crushes the most stout-hearted man. Paradoxically the less his hosts know about their guest's professional and social standing, the better they treat him. It safeguards them against underestimating his importance. To protect themselves against impostors, they devised the biographical calling card (although why a calling card should be taken at face value escapes me). A visitor's first purchase in Japan, therefore, are bilingual name cards—Japanese face, English reverse. Unfortunately the calling card of a Japanese is rarely bilingual; when at the day's end you empty your pockets and stare uncomprehendingly at the Chinese characters, you realize that the system does not benefit *you*.

A box of cards gives out faster than a box of Kleenex on a February day. (On meeting a couple, you also extend a card to the spouse.) Some people collect cards, not necessarily for practical or sentimental reasons; an intrepid young man discovering a foreigner on a train may walk up to him and ask for his card. However, acquaintances-to-be are less interested in the spelling of one's name—most of them prefer to ignore it altogether—than in one's biography. A regular Japanese calling card is an abbreviated who's who listing, complete with affiliations at home and abroad. Although this will seem reasonable enough to the businessman who is judged by the company that keeps him, travelers who do not buy or sell look at this checking system with unconcealed annoyance. If, on the other hand, you have no card, you will attract suspicion. In Japan, freedom from ties makes you an outcast.

In former times, self-introduction was always performed at great length, sometimes at the risk of one's life. On the battlefield enemies would not engage in combat without having informed each other about their precise status. A warrior would seek out a promising foe, step up to him and make his formal acquaintance by exchanging genealogical information, and, "if either found anything to upbraid in the other's antecedents or family history, he did not fail to make loud reference to it, such a device being counted efficacious as a means of disturbing the hearer's sang-froid."[33] This worked fine in the clubby atmosphere of civil wars but on the rare occasion when Japanese had to fight a non-Japanese enemy, the custom spelled disaster for them. The historian F. Brinkley, writing about the first Mongol invasion of Japan in 1274, noted that "it must have been a grim surprise for the polite *samurai* when, in answer to his punctilious proclamation of his names and titles, a mass of unscrupulous Mongols set upon him and hacked him down, instead of the single adversary for whose leisurely and dignified advance he had prepared himself."[34]

Through the years, the Japanese have perfected almost foolproof ways to impress a visitor favorably and take every precaution to avoid contretemps. If it is good form in England to leave a guest alone, it is not in Japan. Not a move of his is left to chance, not a minute's time is left unscheduled. To let him out of sight for a moment is a threat to the Japanese's peace of mind.

This tutelary attitude toward foreigners has a long tradition. The first to complain about it were the Dutch traders who, at the beginning of the seventeenth century, had been permitted to live on Dejima, a microscopic island in Nagasaki Bay. Ostracized for being aliens (they were not allowed to bury their dead in Japanese soil) their treatment at the hands of the Japanese was full of paradoxes. Whenever they left their compound—their prison, as they called it—they brought down upon themselves all the rigors of their hosts' hospitality. In typical Japanese fashion they were honored with the loss of privacy. "They will not leave us alone," wrote one guest with something less than total detachment, "not even when nature obliges us to drop our needs."[35]

Permission to take a walk in the streets of Nagasaki was obtained only after petitioning the authorities. "Leave was granted," one of the Dutch recalled, "provided the captive be accompanied by a certain number of interpreters, and

The Bay of Nagasaki, a page from the travel diary of Nanko Haruki, 1788.

of subaltern officers whose business it is, upon the occasion, to defray whatever expenses of purchases may occur. All these individuals are again attended by several domestics, until their followers amount to twenty-five or thirty persons."[36] These numbers did not include the street urchins who followed the procession, shouting *"Horanda! Horanda!"* which was their way of pronouncing the word Hollander. "But even so," our informant continues, "the train is still far from its complement. Every official holds himself entitled to invite as many of his friends as he pleases to join the party, the whole of which the temporarily liberated Dutchman is bound to entertain."[37]

Today, one comes across similar processions dragging foreign tourists about, perhaps with the difference that the boys are shouting *"Hero! Hero!"* It isn't a case of mistaken hero worship; they are merely pronouncing Hello the Japanese way.

When, in 1854, the Japanese government abandoned its policy of seclusion and opened the country to friendly intercourse with the Barbarians at large, suspicion against them remained as strong as ever. Townsend Harris, the first American to travel in Japan (over a prescribed route) forever complained about what he called "the national principle of concealing everything." He was perpetually vexed by Japanese secretiveness. "I do not think," he wrote, "that any Japanese ever tells the truth, if it can possibly be avoided. He prefers using falsehood when the simple truth would answer just as well."[38] Was it possible that Harris misinterpreted Japanese reticence? Was he unaware of all the indiscretions committed by his compatriots? Did he not know that Perry, speaking before the American Geographical Society in 1856, had blurted out that "the people of America will, in some form or other, extend their dominion and their power until they shall have . . . placed

83

the Saxon race upon the eastern shores of Asia . . . ?"[39]

It rankled in Harris' mind that the simplest geographical facts about the country were withheld from him. A man whose business it was to negotiate a series of treaties supposedly beneficial not only to Japan (he doubted this) but to the entire world, he was treated like a spy, albeit one of ambassadorial rank. "After an incredible amount of talk and difficulty," he wrote in his diary, "the Japanese have given me a map of Yedo (Tokyo). I am not to give it away or suffer it to be copied."[40] A week earlier, he

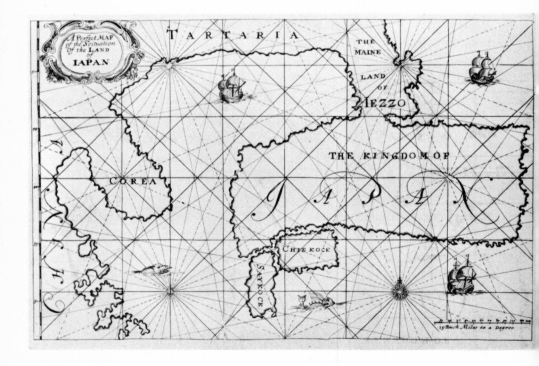

Maps were still top secret at the time of Japan's opening. For navigation in Japanese waters, Perry had to use unreliable charts bought from a Dutchman for $30,000. This "perfect map" that shows Japan as a peninsula, appeared in François Caron's *True Description of the Mighty Kingdoms of Japan and Siam*, 1671.

had noted: "The prince of Shinano tells me that the person who gave maps to von Siebold did not perform the *hara-kiri* but was crucified; and that a number of persons lost their lives by their conduct on that occasion."[41]

Although maps have long been declassified as top secret, the country is by no means an open book. The foreigner who tries to escape the routine of orthodox sight-seeing finds himself immobilized by unexpected obstacles. Mountains become inaccessible, roads impassable, waters dangerous, inns unaccommodating. Japan shuts up like an oyster.

Unfailingly, apologies are tended, explanations offered. No act of hostility is involved, merely an onset of national malaise. Americans with their own long record of distrusting all foreigners ought to be able to sympathize.

The classical landscape of table mountains and conical hills, meandering rivers and villages (practically hidden by trees) can still be found unchanged in today's Japan. From an undated book on imperial mausolea and holy places.

Ladies Last

It is all very well to tell a prospective visitor to Japan not to be overly concerned with native etiquette, to assure him that the Japanese do not expect him to behave according to their code; left to his own devices, he will find that his flashy smile, athletic handshake and stentorian voice, qualities believed irresistible at home, are of no avail in Japan. Much as he welcomes the encounter with a genial people, on close contact he is unable to bridge the cultural gap by an inch.

What is he to do when on his visit to a Japanese house he finds himself in the presence of a superbly dressed woman prostrating herself at his feet? Since her posture does not permit her to look up, his smile goes unnoticed. Her palms are touching the floor and, for want of a receptive hand, his own must remain unshaken. How does a foreigner, he asks himself, enter into the spirit of the occasion? Is he supposed to accept the extraordinary homage? If so, which is the proper way to acknowledge it? Certainly not by placing his foot on her neck. Should he refuse the archaic salutation, go down on his knees and lift her tenderly from the floor? And then—what next? Extend his native greetings—smile, handshake, and hello? A paltry contrast they would make to her extravagant gesture. As luck would have it, on his first collision with Japanese etiquette, his clumsiness stands revealed. What makes the situation downright intolerable for him is the lack of a clue as to whether the woman is a maid or the mistress of the house.

Politeness is an elusive virtue, and the idea that a natural politeness, an unerring sense for doing the right thing in every situation, exists is doubtful in view of our voluminous etiquette books, whose rules are bewilderingly complex. Worse, they are forever changed, amended, and abridged to the dismay of all those aspiring to perfection. Not so in Japan where etiquette leaves nothing to chance or personal interpretation. An inflexible code of behavior makes a Japanese a past master in politeness—that is, as long as he stays on his home ground. The lower his station in life, the stricter the rules.

Rank preoccupies a Japanese no end. Whereas with us only the chief of protocol is supposed to know who precedes whom, such knowledge is indispensable for Japanese who want to get ahead in life. Newspapers record the fluctuations of social ratings, such as whether a government official ranks higher than a physician. "Japanese scholars derive their prestige not from the learning they supposedly have attained but from being members of the government," writes a professor of philosophy, Shunsuke Tsurumi. "The law department of one Imperial University is known to include many scholars who advocate the unconditional abolition of the status system. And yet when they march out of the dining room, they strictly follow the order

89

of court ranks accorded to them."[42] Even in the poorest house privileges are rigidly enforced. Age is honored, but, unlike in our society, a man has precedence over a woman.

Withal, the fortunate recipients of civilities are few: members of the clan, magistrates and teachers. Priests rank low, being regarded as undertakers rather than spiritual guardians. The vast, anonymous mass of people—pedestrians and occupants of public conveyances—are treated with no more consideration than inanimate objects. Yet what are considered bad manners in New York or Paris, may be good manners in Tokyo, and vice versa.

One way to evaluate etiquette would be to measure the amount of energy expended on ceremoniousness. Take such an elementary act as greeting. In former times a gentleman cultivated greeting as assiduously as dancing or making music; an eighteenth-century obeisance amounted to a short version of a ballet. The perfect flourish for lifting the hat was probably as expensive to acquire as a golfer's swing today. Nothing of that art has survived. In the new world even the vestige of a man's greeting, *tipping* his hat, has disappeared. A smile—the smallest coin for buying oneself out of an obligation—and its counterfeit, the smirk, merely mark the borderline between recognition and non-recognition. To bare one's head in greeting, a custom still prevalent in some parts of the world, is looked upon among us as a hangover from the servility of feudal days.

How amazing, therefore, are the greetings the Japanese exchange as a matter of course! When it comes to salutatory attention, they outdo any and all nations. Although they do not necessarily bare their heads in greeting, they stop in their tracks and, as a mere preamble for bowing, unwind their shawls, take off their overcoats, even on the street in the cold of winter. To the uninitiated it looks like preparations for a brawl.

With them, bowing is a way of life. "Oftentimes in the past," we read in a modern etiquette book, "when on a visit and greeting each other, those who met bowed after every few words." One might say that they used bows for punctuation. "But in the present day this is considered too complicated, and after the first salutation is made it is thought better to use only the light bow."[43] Still, bowing deep and copiously is performed with gusto in such unlikely places as public conveyances, railroad stations, and department stores. Since there is little elbowroom, greeters risk being washed away by the torrents of passersby, yet, even with their bows knocked askew, serenity prevails and no stampede, downpour, or blizzard will interfere with their maneuvers. The vigor of their bowing ebbs ever so slightly, to forestall their being caught upright while the opponent is still bent low.

In the olden times, when the occasion called for an obeisance, often only total collapse would do. Bowing correctly meant going down on all fours, in the dust or mud, and entailed a cleaning operation of some magnitude. Nonobservance spelled doom for a man. During the two and a half centuries of unrelieved peace which preceded Japan's opening, *samurai* kept their swordsmanship from getting rusty by butchering those stiff-necks they found wanting in bowing technique.

Their science of good breeding, as Siebold called it, is sedulously practiced in the home where taking leave and welcoming are great occasions for ceremony. "In Japan whenever one's parents are going out or returning, one goes to the door to send them off or to welcome them back."[44] Proliferation is often spurred by a man's need for numerous attendants, for to leave his house unnoticed is nothing short of disgraceful. It makes him feel that he has lived in vain.

There is one occasion when bowing is uncalled-for, and

to the newcomer this can be an unsettling experience. If he meets members of the household in the corridor on his way to the Great Convenience Place or morning bath, they will pass him without returning his greetings, without a sign of recognition. Although they may look at him, they do not see him. It just happens that his unwashedness makes him invisible. Later, when he turns up primped and pinked, greetings will be lavished on him, civility will be thrown into high gear and will whir to his heart's content. There is a time and place for everything.

The machine age spawned a curious subspecies of formal greeting—what might be called the off-bow, or the bow-on-the-bias. It amounts to bowing *away* from the subject of one's homage and was brought about by the introduction of the automobile. It can be observed wherever Japanese are on the point of leaving by car. After the prescribed number of salutations have been exchanged successively in the house, at the entrance, at the gate, in the street, the leave-taking party seated in the car and the motor started, a last vigorous flurry of bowing is still to come. With hosts and domestics lined up on both sides of the car, the occupants now face the problem of returning greetings in badly constricted space. A light bow or a wave of the hand are not polite enough; only a bow from the waist will do. Difficult as it is to bow when seated, it is next to impossible to perform a sedentary *side* bow. The only direction that allows for amplitude is forward and this is the direction in which they bend. The astonished observer is presented with the spectacle of two groups crosshatching the air with deep bows, without facing each other.

A Japanese sees nothing incongruous in these tangential salutations. At the outer moat of the Imperial Palace we find him bowing reverently in the general direction of the emperor's mansion even though the august tenant may

"Coming from the bath," a print,
uncropped, of slender format, by
Torii Kiyomitsu (1735–1785).

be at his seaside villa. During the Occupation, much was made of the peoples' habit of bowing toward the office building that sheltered Douglas MacArthur's brass. This gesture was taken by Americans for an expression of profound reverence, whereas in truth to most Japanese a bow is a perfunctory act, as cheerless as paying income tax. At any rate, it suits them far better than the clammy grip of a hand.

If we are amused by Japanese salutations, the Japanese are not by ours. Disliking as they do to be touched, they find a handshake nothing short of disgusting. Except in their ways with children, they abhor the tenderness of certain body contacts—arms linked, fingers interlaced, a hand caressing a cheek or stroking hair, or even such spontaneous gestures as helping someone across the street, up a staircase, past a door. Among adults, all these little tokens of love and courtesy are unknown. Confucius laid down the word that men and women "should not pass things directly from hand to hand," and his word became law in Japan.

Usages are, of course, immune to criticism within the society in which they are practiced, especially when their raison d'être is forgotten. "It is the essence of usages to have lost their meanings," wrote Ortega y Gasset; "we not only greet each other without knowing what we are doing when we shake hands in salutation—hence, we do it inhumanly—but, in consequence, we do it against our will, wish or pleasure. In addition to being unintelligible, it is an action that is involuntary, sometimes countervoluntary—a further inhuman characteristic."[45] We would have a hard time explaining to a Japanese why we shake hands. The gesture is automatic. We could volunteer the theory that the handshake was born of suspicion—a man grabbed another's hand to see whether he concealed a weapon. But this might only amuse a Japanese who practices *karate*,

94

the art of killing a person with a blow of his *empty* fist.

We smile at the salutations of other nations—the effusive Latin *abraço* (the embrace where men for minutes affectionately, if absentmindedly, pat each other's back), the heel-clicking of the Prussians, the nose-rubbing and assorted gestures of exotic peoples—all the while flattering ourselves that a *warm* handshake is supreme in all its implications. That handshake has come a long way since the time when it was a sign of distrust. It now figures on our medals, postage stamps and patriotic posters, symbolizing honesty, faith, equality—all expressed by mere epidermal contact. A handshake combined with a soulful gleam in the eye abrogates any wordy self-introduction. It seals a business deal by substituting for the small print in the contract. Yet, to a Japanese, the handshake is odious, and the orgies of handshaking indulged in by our politicians strike him as foolish.

The first imperial handshake as described by a witness has all the flavor of an expiatory sacrifice: "The incident of the emperor of Japan advancing toward General Grant and shaking hands, becomes a historic event of consequence, and as such I note it. The manner of the emperor was constrained, almost awkward, the manner of a man doing a thing for the first time, and trying to do as well as possible. After he had shaken hands with the General, he returned to his place, and stood with his hand resting on his sword, looking on at the brilliant, embroidered, gilded company, as though unconscious of their presence. Mr. Bingham advanced and bowed, and received just the faintest nod in recognition."[46]

In the early days of enforced contact with the Western barbarians, when moral principles had not yet given way to considerations of expediency, clasping the hand of the wrong person meant risking one's life. Foreign visitors of

In Japan swords are still venerated in the age of automatic weapons. They are superior in workmanship to Damascene and Toledan products. A page from a book on sword points.

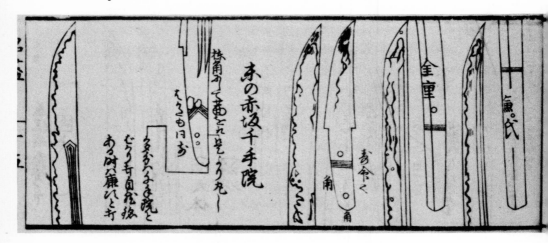

rank, relying purely on their own native manners, probably never realized the potential hazards of mixing socially with the Japanese. When Grant and his wife arrived at the Imperial Palace, writes Ki Kimura (*Japanese Literature, Manners and Customs*), "they entered the room in the Western fashion, the Emperor walking beside Mrs. Grant, and the General escorting the Empress. The Confucian tradition, which forbade the sitting together of the opposite sexes after the age of seven, was still strong in Japan and the story has it that Motoda Eifu, an Imperial lecturer, and others, carried daggers concealed under their clothing, and kept a sharp eye on the General, resolved to stab him should he so much as take the Empress' hand."[47]

In the past, striking power and vigilance were of elementary consideration; a dagger was regarded as indispensable as a fountain pen today. "A pocket poniard was always carried in the bosom," Dr. Inazo Nitobe, the author of *Bushido, the Soul of Japan,* told an American audience in a lecture on Japanese etiquette. Not only men were equipped with the deadly instrument; "samurai daughters

96

were taught to use weapons, not so much on their enemies as on themselves, when there was danger of disgrace."[48] Even in the face of death, etiquette had to be scrupulously observed, dying having always been the supreme occasion for the display of good breeding. As part of their education, explained Dr. Nitobe, Japanese girls were taught all sorts of dodges. "If time allowed, a woman had first to tie her lower limbs firmly together with one of the numerous small sashes which are part of her clothing, the object being to keep the limbs decently composed during the throes of accompanying mortal agony. Moreover, she was taught exactly where to strike in the throat or breast." And he added facetiously, "perhaps this was the only lesson in anatomy that girls were taught in the olden times."[49]

To the uncouth foreigner the spectrum of Japanese po-

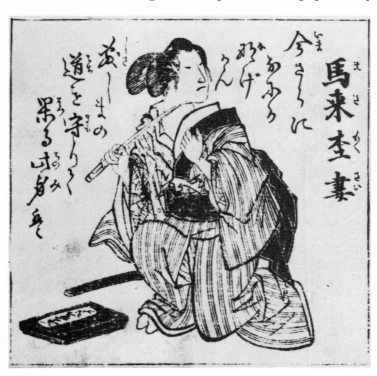

From *Hundred Renowned Women of Recent Times,* 1881.

liteness seemed dizzyingly complex. The dangers incurred in trusting his native etiquette are demonstrated in another episode. In 1872, while touring the southern provinces, the emperor visited the foreign school in the castle town of Kumamoto. One of the teachers, the wife of an American captain, presented him with a bouquet of flowers she had grown from seeds brought from home. To a Japanese, a bunch of cut flowers was then and still is an outlandish contrivance. A bouquet, wrote Lafcadio Hearn, is "but a vulgar murdering of flowers, an outrage upon the color-sense, a brutality, an abomination."[50] Clearly, to offer cut flowers, especially American ones, to the god-emperor was not a good idea. It was worse than grossness; it amounted to lèse majesté, if not blasphemy.

A gracious act of clemency saved the sinner and her case was dismissed. Whichever way one looks at it, it does credit to the emperor to have let the teacher go unpunished. The Japanese chronicler who recorded the incident, ends on a note of cautious commiseration. "Eventually," he writes, "it was decided that inasmuch as the woman was a foreigner practicing a foreign custom no harm had been done."[51]

If Americans experience difficulties in taking the hurdles of Oriental etiquette, Japanese are sometimes driven to desperation by the topsy-turviness of Western manners. Almost everyone has met at some party or other that crushed wallflower, the solitary Japanese—taciturn, sullen, the image of the misanthropist. His disapproving countenance hides inexpressible misery. Everything around him fills him with dismay. His hostess, trying to put him at ease, merely aggravates his torment. Never having acquired a taste for what we call polite conversation (a Japanese refers to his wife as *gu-sai,* stupid wife), he cannot find relief in talk. Informality unnerves him, and his inability to judge the

亞墨利加
女人

His sure sense for accuracy deserts a Japanese artist when he portrays an exotic subject. The American woman, as seen by Yoshitora, has slit eyes, a classical Japanese nose and barbarian locks topped by a somewhat disheveled Indian headdress.

social standing of a foreigner drives him to distraction. Whatever virtues he calls his own he often fails to show for lack of knowing who's who. The more he has been exposed to Occidental manners, the more he comes to appreciate his own. "The trouble is that I don't know when and where to show *enryo* (respect) in American life. You never can be sure," groaned a Japanese scholar back from a year in the States.[52]

Another Japanese resident, an engineer in his late thirties, when asked what he most disliked about America, answered "equality between men and women." "American women are awful," he added, "so unfeminine."[53]

He had a point there. American women are tall, taller than most Japanese men, at any rate. They are loud and self-assertive. They do not walk with their toes turned in. Neither do they kneel before their husbands. "A Japanese," explained the interviewers of our unhappy man (his remarks were duly recorded by a team of American psychol-

It is still good form to go down on all four when greeting, offering or receiving a present. The miniature pine tree is a traditional New Year's gift. Drawing by Ichirûsai Hiroshige (1797–1858).

ogists engaged in a study of the Japanese mind), "normally defines femininity in terms of submissive behaviour." American women, lacking submissiveness, needs must appear to him defeminized "while he in turn feels desexed." No wonder that the very thought of what *we* refer to as chivalry makes a Japanese man ill. His viewpoint was graphically expressed by a prefectural governor back from an educational visit to the States—"Americans make love from the waist up, whereas we Japanese prefer it the other way."[54]

In Japan, a well-bred woman will give up her seat in the streetcar to a man as a matter of course. Her age, or for that matter his age, is of little account; etiquette is inflexible and not subject to personal interpretation. If *she* is offered a seat by a man, young or old, she will not accept it, as any foreigner may learn to his chagrin. Not only is his offer ignored, the stares of the passengers plainly convey the enormity of his faux pas. "What is shocking in one country might be considered commonplace in another," charitably explains an English-language etiquette book; "lacking an understanding of such differences, visitors to Japan have inadvertently and unintentionally shocked the sensibilities of many Japanese."[55] Japanese women abroad suffer a great deal from being exposed to national habits that are the opposite of theirs. Even after living in the United States for years, many "cannot quite reconcile themselves to being waited on by men, feeling a faint sense of impropriety about it."[56]

The best way to come face to face with the unadvertised aspects of Japanese etiquette is to take a plunge into the maelstrom of a local train. In Japan, public means of transportation do the job of school buses and, consequently, are taxed beyond their capacity. Although the Japanese have an unconquerable distaste for being touched by strangers, they vigorously rub elbows in a crowd. Yet even in the cramped space of a subway or bus the niceties of etiquette are scrupulously observed. Males of all ages are comfortably seated, *samurai*-fashion, knees spread wide apart. Some of them take up space for two, while mothers, mothers-to-be, grandmothers, and great-grandmothers are left standing. Often an entire mule-column of women festooned with babies and burdens board a car to find standing room only. Too short of stature to hang onto a strap, the women roll and reel to the jolts of the train, and, as the loads add momentum to their clumsy movements, their plight rouses hilarity among their fellow passengers.

Foreigners unversed in the subtleties of Oriental psychology, haunted by glowing, if deceptive, hometown memories—homely woman entering a crowded bus, one dozen men jumping to their feet—are mystified. They assume that a nation fond of baseball and Hollywood movies

From *Ancient and Modern Various Usages of Tokio Japan,* 1885.

also shares the cult of woman. Alas, this betrays faulty reasoning and a maudlin mind. Worse, they cannot refrain from commenting unfavorably on folkways beyond their comprehension. "A man will not be likely to offer a seat, even to a woman in her tenth month," wrote D. J. Enright in his *World of Dew;* "students and school boys are the most determined seat-seekers and the most tenacious seat-keepers."[57]

The young seat-seekers are far from behaving improperly; on the contrary, they are asserting their birthright. In Japan, the honorable brat is admired, indeed, fêted for his ruthlessness. Appropriately enough the Japanese have a Boys' Festival instead of a Mother's Day. On the fifth day of the fifth month, boy-studded families fly, from tall bamboo poles, paper streamers in the shape of a carp, one for each son. In the strong wind, the paper carp—which often attains a length of several yards—gives a good imitation of a real carp swimming upstream, past whirlpools and cascades. To the Japanese the carp is the very symbol of the fighting spirit. "Because of its strength and its determination to overcome all obstacles it is held to be a fitting example for growing boys, typifying ambition, energy, strength, perseverance," proclaims the *Official Guide* to Japan. "This is the fundamental idea of the festival: the encouragement of manliness, the overcoming of life's difficulties, and consequent success."[58]

On public vehicles, every day is Boys' Festival. Fathers beam with pride at the young carps wiggling their way to a seat. The older they are, the swifter and more powerful their dive—a mob of thousands storming a train or a ferry with apocalyptic force is an awesome spectacle. Hobbled by their kimono, precariously balanced on their clogs, women go down like tenpins. Nobody stops to help them back to their feet. They lie sprawling, waiting for the herd to pass, to collect their bundles and footwear. "There had been talk of and books have been read on the American respect for women and the policy of 'ladies first,' *but the actual situation could not be visualized,*" writes the historian Kimura.[59] (Our italics.)

In Japan, a boy's ego is developed early. The girl child is told to walk behind her brother and to defer to his whims and wishes. By sleeping in the same room with his parents, the baby boy gets an inkling of his future privileges. Thus, when playing with other children he may give proof of

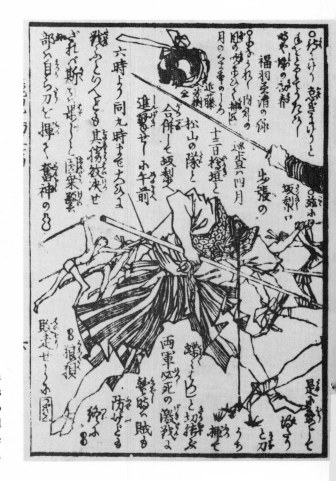

During the Kagoshima Rebellion (1877), European-style uniforms transformed Japanese soldiers into slim six-footers. Traditional sword play and battle gore prevailed—see severed head at the top of the page.

his knowledge; "in rural areas," noted Embree, "children playing house may imitate their parents not only in sweeping and cooking but also in love-making."[60] The mother herself instills in her sons aggressiveness and a sense of superiority. In the years preceding television and movies, when she had to do her own programming, she recited to them stories of military exploits, almost before they left her breast. (Some still suckle at the age of seven.) "Does a little booby cry for an ache?" the mother said. "What will you do when your arm is cut off in battle? What when

you are called to commit *hara-kiri?*" (Nitobe, *Bushido.*)[61]
The bravery displayed by Japanese soldiers in the Pacific
War indicates that the mothers' words fell on eager ears.

Today the mother is more likely to have her mind occupied with P.T.A. meetings or Chinese cooking lessons and
probably doesn't fancy a one-armed son. Still, the great
tradition of Japanese virtues persists, celebrated on big and
small screens where one can view any hour of the day, and
far into the night, the counterpart of the Western gunman,
the *samurai,* cutting a swath of death through the boobies.

Paradoxically the child is taught not to touch other people, a taboo that sometimes extends even to dolls—a collection of dolls is something to be looked at but not handled.
By the time he is an adolescent, any warmth he may have
felt toward his fellow man has given way to chilly politeness. Not even in his speech does he permit himself to be
intimate; the husband addressing his wife does not, as a
rule, use her first name. Public display of affection is ab-
horred. Kissing was formerly known from hearsay and
book-reading only, and little understood ethically and me-
chanically. "When the word appeared in grammar school
textbooks, the teacher who very often could not visualize
the act himself, might give such inaccurate explanations
as 'to suck with the mouth' or 'to lick with the lips.' "[62]
Deleted by censorship from all imported films until World
War II, the kiss now occupies considerable space and time
on the wide screen of moving-picture houses, yet for all we
know, Japanese audiences watching a torrid embrace may
feel much the same way children do when watching copu-
lating animals.

In their epic, if unspectacular, struggle with alien concepts of etiquette—from the moist handshake to the even
moister kiss—the Japanese have been unsuccessful in cop-
ing with that foremost ingredient of Western politeness:

"An Interrupted Embrace." (The man is in the center.) Woodcut by Sugimura Jihei Masataka, ca. 1685.

punctuality. Whatever our chances for "understanding" them, it is profitable to examine some basic differences between their outlook on time and ours.

Thrifty in many respects, the Japanese are lavish with time. While it is true that stationmasters go overboard in their cult of punctuality, the better part of the traveling public remains unaffected by it. I have known some gentlemen of the old school with a fine disregard for time schedules. When traveling, they are benignly ignorant about departure and arrival times; they never give the impression of wanting to *catch* a train. Carrying no more baggage than a fan and a briefcase and disdaining the send-off by families or greeting committees, they like to stroll, as it were, into a station to contemplate leisurely their chances for

107

transportation, much as a Frenchman stops in front of a restaurant to scrutinize the day's specials. To them, railroad stations are oases of timelessness, like those moving-picture houses that advertise "continuous performances."

"The Japanese take so little interest in time that they are far from entitled the modern nation," says a quaintly worded report of the Japanese Commission for Unesco; "they have the custom of being behind time appointed."[63]

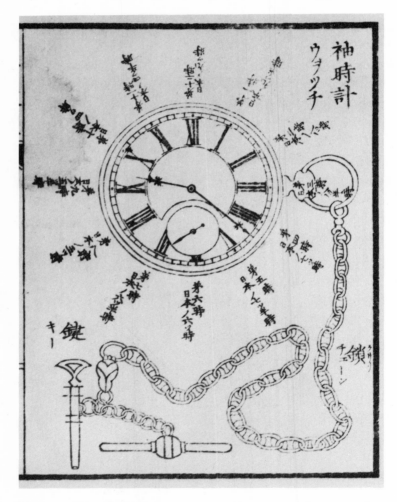

Since traditional Japanese garments have no pockets, watches were originally carried in the sleeves of the kimono.

Although most Japanese carry a timepiece, they are not its slaves. They are not anxious, as we are, to "save" time, as if seconds and hours were pennies and dollars. Hence, the time-conscious foreigner who makes his home in Japan finds life painfully unhurried. Tradesmen are in the habit of ignoring delivery dates; deadlines are seldom honored, postponements are the rule. Yet none of these shortcomings touch upon the specific nature of Japanese unpunctuality. It happens that the Japanese are not late out of laziness, for their proneness to being late is matched by an equally vexing proneness to being early. In other words, people think nothing of showing up hours before time— if you invite Japanese to dinner at eight, be prepared to see them arrive at six.

In their code of behavior, to be immoderately early for a date stands for polite anticipation. To arrive at the appointed hour could easily be taken for indifference. Such eagerness to show affection would no doubt be most touching were it not also quite likely that on the very same occasion, other dinner guests arrive two hours late. To bridge the interval of four hours between the arrivals demands a temper few Westerners possess. "Being behind time appointed," the Unesco report elaborates, "is little with consideration (among rural Japanese). Besides, when a late-comer appears, he hardly makes an excuse for being late; while the other waits for him is not nervous about being kept waiting so long."[64] One does of course also come across the punctilious Japanese, yet his basic attitude toward time may not necessarily be different from his nonpunctual countryman for, although he makes a point of arriving on time, he may entertain no thought about the proper time for *leaving*. "As for visiting, the Japanese people seem to lack temperance," says the melancholy report.[65]

The overnight guest who won't take a hint can be dislodged only through the power of charms. A knot tied in his underclothes may do the trick, or the placing of lukewarm ashes under his bedding—a sort of tepid hotfoot. If these do not work, "stand a broom on end in the room next to your guest's room, and laying out a pair of sandals before it say in a whisper—There now, do please, go away quickly."[66]

One Japanese book warns foreigners not to take casual invitations seriously. "In most cases such invitations do not mean anything at all. Those words are spoken for the sake of courtesy. If a foreigner thinks that he is really invited and goes to visit his Japanese friends, he will be greatly disappointed and embarrassed, as the host is not expecting him."[67]

For reasons known to the Japanese only, the rules are not reversible. "Foreigners must be prepared to receive calls from Japanese friends at any time, day or night."[68] Above all, one must learn to yield to the woman visitor. Modesty dictates that she tarry in the door and ignore all summons to enter the house, lingering forever in the entrance, door ajar. If this is a calamity in the cold of winter, it is equally intolerable in summer when mosquitoes are queuing up at the door, waiting for admittance. Alas, one is allowed neither to grab her and haul her inside nor to slam the door in her face. Moreover, when cold or heat wins out against affectation and she reluctantly crosses the threshold, a new situation with new duties arises. "Once a guest enters the house, tea and cake must be served, and meals (sic) have to appear if it is mealtime." Nobody is pulling our leg; checking with the Unesco report, we learn that "even when the guest has come unexpectedly, and not on invitation, it is customary to offer a meal . . ."[69] We have to be satisfied with the behaviorist's dictum that customs are impervious to logic.

In the early stages of his initiation to native social life, when his desire for privacy is keenest, a foreigner may spend time and energy inventing ruses to defeat the polite schemes of the Japanese. If he happens to live in a Japanese-style house, his chances for keeping out uninvited visitors are poor. Like the diabolical Dappertutto in *Tales of Hoffmann,* they insinuate themselves from everywhere. They seem to emerge from bedding closets, from the floor, from the vapors of the bath, the scariest ones being outdoor apparitions. A Japanese garden with its trompe l'oeil perspective is quite tricky in itself, yet when one suddenly makes out a motionless stranger among the camellia bushes, one longs for solid walls, don't-disturb signs, and people who can read them. The supreme outrage is the neighbor's brat who has climbed a tree and from his perch follows one with the cold eye of the Serpent in Paradise.

The correct thing, in fact, the only possible thing to do is to say: Please come in.

A House for the Summer

As a rule, we do not paint moustaches on Mona Lisa or remodel a piece of sculpture that has ceased to give us pleasure. Works of art, we tacitly agree, are not to be tampered with. A house, on the other hand, is fair game for the amateur; an architect's brainchild, it inspires no awe. To people in an industrial society, the house is little more than a commodity of which they easily tire, like a child of his toys. Whereas in the Old World it is not unusual for a house to serve a dozen generations—and serve them well in its original form—in our country such longevity is rare. To lessen the boredom that springs from mechanization, we remake and remodel our houses with such dogged determination that it seems as though they were built with that very purpose in mind.

Among the houses of the Western world, none leads a more precarious existence than the American house. It barely survives from one blood transfusion—performed by interior designers or, more thriftily, by the do-it-yourself inhabitant—to the next. The staggering number of "improvements" a house is able to put up with attest to the permanence of the infirmity. The patent medicines advertised and editorialized in the pages of housekeeping and home-decorating magazines, in special newspaper sections and reams of books, do not cure the illness, but the treatment offers some people a welcome distraction. To others, however, who cannot bear the thought of turning over their premises to a crew of beauticians; who dread the ordeal of reupholstering their furniture and see no humor in cartoons of housewives disputing housepainters on the color of a wall; who find Venetian blinds and window curtains equally dowdy, a house—any house—that promises to function without periodical recourse to surgery would seem the answer to their prayers. The Japanese house—more precisely, the traditional Japanese house, a venerable institution which has been the object of much admiration and occasionally of scorn—is but one of the houses that have proved immune to the fashions of the day.

It is a house turned outside in, except that there never was much of an outside. There are no windows to look out from or into and consequently no window curtains. No carpets or rugs eclipse the floor; no chairs, no beds encroach on its void. Apart from the annual replacement of the floor mats, the house is near-immutable. Long regarded as the conceit of a nation of practical jokers, of late the Japanese house has been looked upon as a triumph of ingenuity, indeed, a work of art.

The good word about it spread slowly. When Commodore Perry got his foot into Japan's sliding door, the Japanese house caused not a ripple of excitement, still less of praise. To wit, we have Perry's own disillusioned account. The first and probably only house he visited belonged to the mayor of a small town; if it was not a showpiece, it was a home no Japanese needed to be ashamed of. "The interior," notes the official *Narrative of the Expedition,* "was quite unpretentious, consisting of a large room, spread out with soft mats, lighted with oiled paper windows, hung with rudely executed cartoons, and furnished with the usual red-colored benches."[70]

Perry does not seem to have gotten much of a briefing in Washington, at least not on the daintier aspects of Japan's civilization. Neither does he seem to have been a keen observer. What he pleased to call "rudely executed cartoons" were *kakemono,* painted scrolls, the pride and treasure of every household. What he took to be oiled paper was the incomparable rice paper. If anything, he might have called it creamy, but there is nothing oily about it. It is dry and translucent like the wings of a moth.

The "red-colored benches" played him a perspective trick. For one thing, contemporary Japanese paintings show Perry as a giant, if only because all Westerners seemed exceedingly tall by Japanese standards. For another, Perry's view of the interior amounted no doubt to a sort of bird's-eye view. Had he deigned to sit down on the matted floor —obviously neither the cut of his uniform nor his exalted rank permitted this—he might have recognized the benches for what they were: tables. We can only hope that he did not commit the faux pas of *sitting* on them.

Surely all Japanese houses look humble to people who regard ostentation a civic virtue. Although in Perry's time

The traditional Japanese house antedates our so-called modern architecture by several centuries. Skeleton structure, open plan, sliding walls have only recently entered our architecture, while removable walls and resilient floors are still in the future.

Japanese life was often on a level that we consider a subsistence minimum, it would be a mistake to think of the Old Japan in terms of endemic poverty. In Japan, poverty often comes close to a state of grace, akin to the frame of mind induced by a monastic life. Some Japanese—especially the well-off—are quite voluble on the subject and argue with warmth the merits of being poor. A platoon of servants and a limousine or two do not impair their devotion to a fastidiously cultivated penury.

The whimsical Japanese habit of concealing prestige and wealth behind a humble front has remained unchanged down to our time. Residential streets are quite unlike ours—innocent of sidewalks and front lawns, with only a cursory pavement. In their confining narrowness they resemble our country lanes except that they are bordered by solid fences of bamboo and wood, ingeniously constructed in a hundred patterns. The fences never look forbidding; they make one feel curious rather than unwanted. "The walls with their regularity of appearance," wrote Ensign Edward Yorke McCauly, one of Perry's diarists, "with the large quantity of trees and plants peeping over them, give the whole a *home-ey* sort of look, as though there might be something inside the establishment, that would be found good for the inner man."[71] Today McCauly would be listed as a security risk. His wistful words betray his plight of being reduced to living in a pillory of a house, with curtains transparent and doors unlocked, forever exposed to the neighbors' inquisitive eyes.

The Japanese house has defied dispassionate analysis. From the lukewarm notices of the earliest Western chroniclers—the Jesuit missionaries and Dutch merchants in the sixteenth and seventeenth centuries—to the panegyrics of contemporary travelers, it represents a stout paradox. Taken by many to be the most elegant shelter ever designed

for man, it also marks the furthest departure from common sense. For all its stylized poverty, it is a dream house, frivolous in plan, frail of build. In the lighthearted words of novelist Tanizaki, "we first spread a parasol to throw shadow on the earth, and in the shadow we put together a house."[72] To the Japanese, shade is more vital than warmth and food. Although they take great pride in their solar ancestry and made a red-hot sun their national emblem, in everyday life they shun the sun's rays. Men and women strive for extreme pallor of skin. A suntan strikes them as only slightly less barbarous than the war paint of savage tribes. A spot of shade, the whiff of a breeze—or, for want of these, an umbrella and a fan—are all a true Japanese asks from life in the way of *confort*. At least, so

From Arnoldus Montanus' *Atlas Japanennsis*, 1670.

we are told. If his parasol-turned-house does not function the way we think it should, it is nevertheless functional in a higher sense.

It just happens that the Japanese attitude toward shelter is at variance with ours: their idea of the perfect house is a summer house (much as our idea of the perfect car is a convertible). Every wretched city hovel aspires to be a pleasure pavilion—and miraculously succeeds. If the Japanese ever felt like defending their folly, they could quote a famous architectural recipe handed down from a fourteenth-century philosopher, Yoshida Kenko: "A house should be built with the summer in view. In winter one can live anywhere but a poor dwelling in summer is unbearable."[73] When we talk contemptuously of "paper houses," we are seldom aware that our houses match theirs in flimsiness and inflammability. Europeans, conditioned to thick-walled constructions, think little of our wooden crates that are carried away by floods or take off like kites in a tornado. It is in our philosophy of shelter that we differ from the Japanese—or rather our lack of such philosophy.

The Japanese house of old has recaptured, if not Paradise, at least some of the aroma of its premises. Perhaps only a people who never heard of Original Sin can conceive of a *sensuous* house, and by sensuous I do not mean the whorish trappings of "interior decoration." A Japanese room is as chaste as a seashell, so much so indeed that we have come to look at it as the quintessence of austerity. Yet in the Orient one finds austerity perfectly compatible with voluptuousness. In fact, they complement each other; it is not by accident that many refinements of Japanese domestic architecture were invented by monks. Among the most felicitous features is the *tatami* floor. "The floors of their houses," wrote Arnoldus Montanus three hundred years before our time, "are Matted all over

Tatami maker. In the background a pile of finished *tatami*.

very curiously, and that they may tread the softer, stuft with Quilt, which indeed, are rather their Couches or Beds."[74] The Elizabethans probably would have relished such luxury. To the Victorians, on the other hand, it was quite a shock to learn that the Japanese house was one big bed—Captain Brinkley, R.A., a historian who did not mince words when describing gory battle scenes, was appalled at the thought of a Japanese house at bedtime. "A Japanese residence," he wrote, "promotes immodesty and therefore immorality; for in the stifling atmosphere all covering at night becomes unendurable, while, at the same time, paper sliding doors are quite ineffective to segregate one room from another."[75]

There is more to *tatami* than meets the eye. They are not just mats but mattresses of rushes woven over a wooden frame, with a mat sewn on top. Their dimensions never vary. Three feet wide, six feet long, and at least two inches thick, they form throughout the house a continuous pavement that yields ever so slightly underfoot. Although a mat represents the minimum sleeping surface for one person, in practice the allotment is far more generous. At night, thickly wadded quilts, called *futon,* and wadded coverlets are taken out of the quilt closet and placed on the floor. "Should the guest find the absence of a spring-mattress rather distressing," the *Official Guide* helpfully remarks, "he may alleviate his discomfort by requiring the maid to spread two or three quilts for him to lie on."[76] An attentive maid will pile quilt upon quilt until the lair looks worthy of a *Sardanapal.*

The spreading and hauling up of *futon* is simplicity itself. In the household of a *samurai* everybody had to make

A hard square pillow, the flattest of quilts, a whiff of warmth from a brazier are about all the comforts to be expected in a monastery.

his own bed and, according to Miss Vining—our contemporary source for imperial intramural customs—it is still the princesses' duty to take out and put away their *futon*. "The room," she writes, "is empty and ready for any kind of use during the day. It is a wonderful way to save space."[77] In the absence of bedsteads and bedrooms, one is free to choose any nook that seems auspicious for a good night's rest. Besides, *futon* are expendable. If the need arises to put up a large party overnight, *futon* can be spread thin.

But it is not just in utilitarian principles that the Japanese excel; they have a knack for infusing poetry, even magic, into routine performances and routine situations

Color woodcut by Kitagawa Utamaro (1753–1806).

which hold no charms for us. The bath is one of them, sleep is another. The crowning soporific touch of the Japanese bed is a tent as ethereal as it is sumptuous. Manifestly intended to keep out mosquitoes, it has a hypnotic power of inducing pleasant dreams. Unlike the Mediterranean variety of mosquito net which droops in thick folds from one central point in the ceiling, this one is a rectangular box of starched netting. Its four panels—which trail on the floor like the train of a robe—and the flat, equally transparent top hang on silk cords from hooks set in the framework of the house. The misty walls of this tent are dyed the color of green sea-foam, or shaded from blue to

123

white like water in a pool, and resemble, as Pierre Loti noted, an immense aquarium with drowned people at its bottom.

Alas, the Japanese arrangement for the night finds little favor with the brand of traveler turned out by the tourist industry today. A deplorer rather than an explorer, he finds sleeping on the floor but one degree removed from rolling in the gutter, a night without the moral support of four legs utter degradation. He considers furniture a prerequisite of an advanced civilization. The bed he regards as the bedrock of marriage, a bed-frame the only dignified frame for the events of birth and death. He is surprised no end to hear that the Western bed has licentious connotations in Japan.

Among the first to purchase beds were brothel-keepers. Open-minded by necessity, they were willing to try the daring and absurd as long as it promised to benefit their trade. The wooden sarcophagus must have appeared to them no less exotic than a horse-drawn carriage (which it somewhat resembles, built as it is on the lines of a wagon, with metal springs to boot, should the going get rough). Its four legs, however, made sense—the space between bedstead and floor accommodated a convenience which early Japanese illustrations of beds never failed to emphasize: a chamber pot. The buoyant mattress was another source of wonder, and so were the pillows, deep and downy, threatening suffocation.

Tokyo's first Western-style hotel, opened in 1867, offered beds as a matter of course. Other hotels followed suit, mostly to satisfy the wishes of foreigners and the curiosity of Japanese clients, but the Western bed never quite displaced the traditional sleeping arrangement at home. "Beds were adopted not for their innate comfort (if any), but for prestige reasons because they were expensive to

The Western bed, explained.

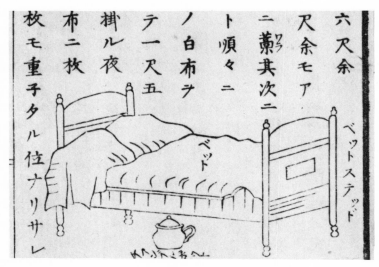

枚モ重子タル位ナリサレ 布二枚 掛ル夜 テ一尺五 ノ白布ヲ ト順々ニ 二薦其次ニ 尺余モア 六尺余

ベッド

ベットステッド

own," writes D. L. Philippi in his *Letters from Harajuku;* "to sleep in a bed was like owning a Cadillac. The bed never sprouted roots, and remained a curiosity and extravaganza." Among newly wed couples it is the fashion to spend the honeymoon in a Western-style hotel—usually in the ancient and dilapidated sort found in mountain resorts —to seek adventure in the unwonted softness of a creaky bed.

Until the advent of Westernization, life on the domestic scene was enacted at the lowest altitude, and, to this day, wherever *tatami* form a common ground, the floor of a traditional room is table, desk, and bed. Western furniture with its towering shapes upset aesthetics as well as manners by entailing, literally, new horizons. The worst offender was the chair.

Unlike sleeping in beds, sitting on chairs requires aptitude and training. To sit for hours with legs dangling, or even with the feet firmly planted on the ground, is torture to the Japanese. Only when their hams touch the floor are

125

they at ease. (To be sure, some city people are inured to chairs and share the foreigners' difficulty in sitting the native way. Whether such difficulty is physical or mental, it contradicts the experience of those Japanese who, after living for years in Western countries, happily go home to their *tatami*.)

Had the Japanese seen any merit in chairs, they could have adopted them from China. The fact that they didn't is significant in view of their notorious weakness for copying foreign inventions. Instead, they waited a thousand years until, bemused by the way things were going in the world, they acquired once and for all the trappings of the barbarians. Of late, much has been made of the "schizophrenic" life of a nation that has taken to Western clothes, Western food, and Western architecture without wanting to make a clean break with the past. We are amazed at the ease with which a Japanese reverts to the customs and comforts of his ancestors the moment he returns to his home. We accuse him of weakness when, in truth, the bond with his past assures him a moral strength that we do not possess. Even physically, we are not his match. Long before middle-age creeps up on us, our bodies have been weakened by creature comforts. To buttress our tottering physique we resort to an arsenal of "supports" and crutches: arm- and foot-rests, vibrating, rocking, contour- and health-chairs (*sic*).

Some delayed optimists hope to regain control over their limbs by turning to yoga and covet mastery of the lotus position as ardently as an honorary degree from a university. Alas, habitual chair-sitters who try to sit unsupported do not always succeed. Their descent to the *tatami* floor is felt by them, if not as a moral decline, as an unwelcome concession to the archaic customs of a reputedly modern nation. Deprived of scaffolding, they simply disintegrate.

A hero of the Meiji Era (1868–1912). From a poetry book.

For all his complacency, Perry was amazed at the lissomeness of the Japanese and paid them a true, if supercilious,
compliment. "They all showed a wonderful elasticity of
muscle and suppleness of joint which could only have been
acquired by a long practice, and reminded one of those
skillful contortionists or clowns, who exhibit their caou-
tchouc accomplishments to the wonderment of the specta-
tors."[78] It probably never dawned on him that it was their
chairless life that helped them preserve the nimbleness of
childhood.

The finer points of the Japanese way of sitting usually
escape the non-Japanese. "In the correct sitting posture,"

127

explains a modern etiquette book intended for foreigners, "the big toes are placed one on top of each other beneath the body. A man's knees are placed about three or four inches apart, a woman's close together."[79] Since sitting on one's toes is an achievement not easily accomplished by Westerners—at least not for any length of time—their behavior is usually allowed some latitude. A Japanese man may sit cross-legged, as do men in other chairless civilizations, but, says our book, "such easy posture must never be used in Japanese clothes or in front of a person of high position."[80] Woman, however, is out of luck since kneeling is much too becoming to her. *Her* reward for observing decorum is calloused ankles. Moreover, the correct posture, it has been pointed out by its critics, is injurious to the body. It interferes with the growth of the legs; it causes a prevalence of bowlegs among Japanese women.

Such arguments fail to move a true-bred Japanese. Bowlegs may look unattractive on the giraffe-like foreigners who roam the cities in the summertime, but as far as his own people are concerned, they suit him to perfection. What, he asks with profound skepticism, is there beautiful about long, straight legs?

Anyone who doubts the authenticity of such notions had better turn to writers and poets for corroboration. In a novel written by Tanizaki in 1961, the hero confides to a diary his tender thoughts about his wife's legs: "they bulge out at the calves, and her ankles are not quite trim. But rather than slim, foreign-looking legs, I have always liked the slightly bowed ones of the old-fashioned Japanese women, such as my mother and aunt. Those slender, pipe-stem legs are uninteresting."[81] Pronouncements such as these roundly disprove any frivolous belief that the caprices of Japanese taste can be fathomed by a non-Japanese.

Withal, most foreigners look with a baleful eye upon the

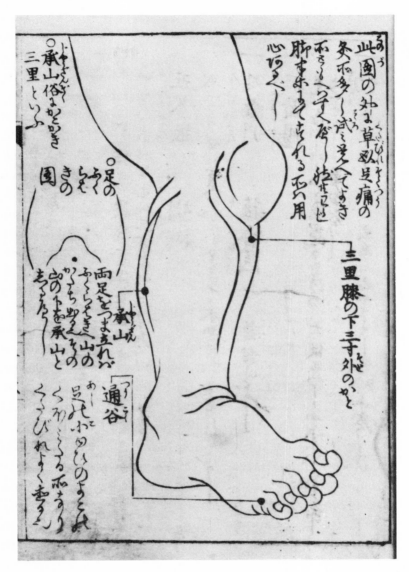

The baroque beauty of the Japanese leg, as illustrated in a book of precautions for travel, dated 1810.

traditional floor. The he-man winces at the prospect of having to remove his shoes; to his mind, unshoeing comes close to cultural rape. The female of the species, deprived of the sting of her heels, feels defenseless and insulted. The trauma of ending up in stocking feet has often spoiled a visitor's welcome, yet unshoeing is only the preamble to his further vexations. As soon as he lowers himself to the matted floor, his legs turn into a formidable stumbling block. Lacking the insect-like facility of the Japanese to fold them in various ways, he finds they behave erratically or go to sleep. Unfortunately the Japanese fail to see the comical side of his predicament. The man who midway through a dinner slides into the supine position is met with stony silence. As in *hara-kiri,* it is disgraceful to fall back-wards.

The Westerner is in for many discoveries and second thoughts. He looks with new eyes at the small child who not only prefers to sit on the floor but protests with all his force against being put into a chair. If sitting on chairs always seemed to him both natural and comme il faut, he now realizes that it is also the *only* way to sit for any length of time.

True to their traditional hospitality, the Japanese have invented a number of artful dodges for the benefit of the foreign visitor. To prop up his flaccid substance, they devised a singular piece of furniture, a sawed-off high chair, with a back and armrests but without legs. Although it does not have the power to rejuvenate its occupant, it permits him to keep up appearances. Another way to cheat the eye is to provide a pit in the floor and to camouflage it with a dining table. This subterfuge is perpetrated in Japanese-style restaurants catering to Westerners, and by those foreign residents who prefer to live in would-be Japanese houses which they endow with touches of their own taste and, inevitably, with "improvements." The pit serves as receptacle for the aggregate legs of the table-guests, permitting them to dine on the floor à la japonaise without depriving themselves of their customary way of sitting.

The *tatami* floor with its built-in challenge to the human physique, inimical to such Western imports as trouser crease and sheer stockings, girdles and garters, is literally the basis and common denominator of traditional Japanese architecture. A lowly thing exquisitely made, *tatami* affords a Japanese the kind of satisfaction our floors cannot give. He likes to compare *tatami* to a meadow, and, without doubt, they do represent to him a bond with nature. Even in the most up-to-date apartment house, each apartment has at least one matted room. At night, when he retires to his fragrant mats, a Japanese finds in them his emotional moorings. From the touch of rice straw he draws the strength to face another day in a world of asphalt.

Detail of a print by Yûsoan. 1669.

Hedonism for the Destitute

One recently published *Guide to the Far East* contains the alarming statement that the Japanese way of bathing is habit-forming, and that foreigners who succumb to it, "consider, with the Japanese, any other system repulsive."[82] It is one thing to indulge in foreign customs, it is quite another to deprecate one's own. The State Department, having shouldered the responsibility, formerly with Thomas Cook and Son, of selecting suitable travel countries for the citizen, ought to go one step further and look into the subversive side of travel.

A few generations ago, things were different. The traveler abroad knew his place and was not perpetually on the verge of losing his national dignity. He did not look at travel as an invitation to debauch. When ladies were still ladies, their reactions to such outlandish institutions as the Japanese bath were unequivocal. One Anna d'A.—she was too modest to reveal her full name—who visited Japan in the 1860s and wrote a book appropriately called *A Lady's*

Visit to Japan, left us a precious snapshot, if only verbal, of a bathing scene. Invited to enter a Japanese house, she did so "without the slightest doubt or hesitation, little prepared for the absurdly indecent scene . . . At the further end of the room [was] a portion partitioned off by a low wall, within which enclosed space numbers of men and women were bathing *in puris naturalibus* [which] reminded me forcibly of a presentation of souls in purgatory I once saw outside a church in Antwerp."[83]

Anna was able to cushion her shock with a morsel of Latin and an elegant reference to art, but a simple sailor has no such mental foxholes to hide in. The dangers seafaring men are liable to encounter, then as now, are described by a diarist of Perry's Japanese expedition. "I went into a bath house," tells Ensign McCauly, "where girls of seventeen, old women, young women, old men were squatting on the stone floor, without rag enough to cover a thumb nail . . . they invited us to join in and take a wash—but I was so disgusted with the whole breed, with their lewdness of manner and gesture, that I turned away with a hearty curse upon them . . ."[84] In modern Japan, a net of relay stations—inns and hotels approved for and by foreigners—assure the most demanding moralist an unbroken succession of wholesome impressions. They all have a clean bill from the Minister of Transportation, the Japanese counterpart of Duncan Hines.

Today as in the past, opinions on the bath are anything but unanimous. Some learned doctor proved to his great satisfaction, I do not remember by what stratagem, that man can live a long life in perfect health without ever taking a bath or, for that matter, without washing himself, and at one time or other, everybody comes across a person who is living proof of the doctor's theory. Among us, the belief in the wholesomeness of bathing is of very recent

date and, what with the shakiness of most of our beliefs, bathing might very well fall into oblivion should somebody come up with a more attractive though not necessarily better idea.

There are proven and approved methods for washing a shirt or a pot but when it comes to cleaning the human epidermis, we disagree on aims as well as needs. Worse, we take exception to all practices that differ from our own. During his six years of residence in Japan, the first American consul Townsend Harris, faithful to his native ways, continued to bathe in cold water—"much to the amazement of the Japanese," as he noted in his diary.[85] To Puritans reared in the masochistic discipline of cold showers, bathing in hot water is anathema; a person who admits to enjoying a hot bath, a voluptuary.

A Japanese would not dream of taking a bath in cold water, all the more as he has plenty of running hot water available. No other country in the world is as liberally provided with natural hot springs. Japan boasts over a thousand medical thermae, and so far nobody has taken the trouble to count the nonmedical ones. To be sure, in some parts of the country, running water, hot or cold, is scarce, yet people do not bathe less frequently because of it. Some bathe several times a day. They go without a meal rather than without a bath. "For the poorest rice farmer and the meanest servant, just as much as for the rich aristocrat, the daily soak in superlatively heated water is part of the routine of every late afternoon," wrote Ruth Benedict.[86]

Basil Hall Chamberlain called bathing *la grande passion* of the Japanese, coming perhaps closest to its true nature. Their bath, it has been said, is primarily a ritual, although few Japanese will agree to this. The word ritual applies

more correctly to their notion of cleanliness which does not stop at the body and its coverings but extends to the house as well. The best known example of this concept is the custom of taking off their shoes before entering a house. While we expend energy and imagination on inventing new methods of cleaning floors, the Japanese solve the problem by not dirtying them in the first place.

Word has reached the most uninformed tourist about this elementary precaution against carrying the filth of the streets into the house, but few of them have ever heard how the Japanese go about taking a bath. For generations the Japanese have tried to wipe out this annoying ignorance. At inns, multilingual notices far from any tone of spoof proclaim the rules in quaint language, and guidebooks are most emphatic on one point: one does not enter

Shuzenji, a spa popular since the ninth century. One of its hot springs gushes forth from the middle of the torrential river that flows through the village.

a Japanese tub unless one is perfectly clean.

This may seem as absurd as sitting down to a meal perfectly sated. Yet what is absurd to us is not necessarily so to a Japanese. Come to think of it—if you are invited to a banquet at the Imperial Palace, you will do well not to arrive on an empty stomach. Prepare for the august occasion by eating a hearty meal, for although the monarch has divested himself of some minor aspects of his godliness, it is still blasphemy to eat in his presence. Anyway, there is nothing paradoxical about bathing in a clean state—it is the only civilized way. Westerners who follow the Japanese custom for any length of time find it most natural. Few, if any, will lapse into their old habit of wallowing in their own dishwater, so to speak.

To the Japanese our very methods of cleaning are dirty, and they are not alone in their idiosyncrasy. "In India the people consider an ordinary tub bath an extraordinarily dirty habit," writes Santha Rama Rau.[87] Devoid of any genuine desire for keeping clean, we mistake our efforts at cleaning for cleanliness itself. To us, cleanliness is not an innate trait but a budgetary item—the responsibility of charwomen, window cleaners, and laundries. It does not occur to us that our *manners* are unclean to the Asians. Indians, for example, share the Japanese distaste for them. "Indians," elaborates Miss Rau, "consider foreigners dirty because they shake hands, wear shoes indoors, eat with knives and forks."[88]

The Japanese rate body cleanliness a concomitant of bathing rather than its motive. Washing, which in our bathing routine is the pith of the matter, in Japan is performed outside the tub. There are no showers; the soaping and scrubbing is followed by repeated dousing with bucketfuls of water. Since the room is empty—except for the tub, which often is a sunken tub—and the slatted floor drains off the water, splashing, rather than being a calamity, adds a note of merriment to the bath. Faithful to the tradition of civilized countries, the Japanese do not practice our custom of putting a tub into a latrine or, what amounts to the same, installing a toilet in the bathroom. Despite their weakness for Western gadgets, they draw the line at our bathroom. Preferring to ignore our bathing arrangements, they also remain totally unacquainted with our bathing *methods*. Most Japanese never see the inside of a Western bathroom, except perhaps in moving pictures. Neither will they—nor indeed we—give much thought to the predicament of a Japanese who is about to take his first bath abroad. It simply does not occur to anybody that he, too, needs instruction, as a couple famous for their hospitality found out to their regret.

A Japanese houseguest of theirs taking his first Western bath in their New York apartment, disinclined as he was to enter the tub without having washed, lathered himself and after some browsing discovered a serviceable substitute for a bucket, whereupon he began to drench himself with many helpings of hot water—from ingrained habit outside the tub. He became aware of, but was left unmoved by, the fact that the water he splashed about was not absorbed by a floor drain but escaped under the closed bathroom door. Not one to reflect on this unusual device, still less given to questioning the merits of foreign arrangements, he finished his bath in leisure, with the composure expected from his race. The point of the story is that his hostess, herself a Japanese, with her manners unimpaired by years of living abroad, was standing all the time behind the door in the corridor, mopping up the water as fast as she could without uttering a sound.

Anyone conditioned to tiled bathroom walls and plate-glass shower stalls might consider an all-wooden room, with walls, ceiling, and floor of unpainted wood, the least likely place for taking a bath. And so, he thinks, is the wooden tub, the classical square type of box with a wooden lid to keep the water from cooling off when not in use. Its velvety smoothness and fragrance give a novice the first inkling that there is a sensuous side to bathing. Compared to the wood's caress, the touch of an enameled tub is frigid. But then Japanese wood is not just ordinary lumber. The stock of a lumberyard is catalogued like books in a library, every board carrying an identification. Like pages of a book, boards cut from the same tree are sold together. And such is the quality of their wood that it is easy to see why they prefer it in its natural state. The very idea of painting or staining it is revolting to them. It is not a matter of taste but a case of vandalism. During the last war people looked on dry-eyed as their cities went up in flames, but they never forgave those American families who lived in requisitioned Japanese houses for covering every inch of woodwork with paint.

In the Japanese bath the scrubbing and dousing serves merely to tune up the body for immersion in water so hot as to be barely tolerable. The trick is to get into the tub fast, with the greatest economy of movement; to glide into the water without rippling its surface. As long as one keeps still, the hot water does not hurt. Submerged to the chin, one crouches in the burial position fashionable the world over in prehistoric times. To call the immersion a soak, as Ruth Benedict does, is an understatement. What takes place in the tub is regeneration, something close to a sacrament. The Christian martyrs who stepped into caldrons of boiling oil with a smile and a prayer on their lips came closest to the sense of fulfillment a Japanese bath bestows on an unflinching soul.

The average Japanese tub is small, for the Japanese are

not only slight of build, they have a singularly high compression quotient. The Sagamiya Inn at Izusan boasts of a *sennimburo,* a thousand people's bath, duly noted in the *Official Guide* to Japan. On measuring it, it turns out to be fifteen by thirty feet, about the size of a New York living room or a small midtown art gallery. As anybody who frequents cocktail parties and gallery openings can attest, such an area is indeed able to absorb an unlimited number of people. And, in a way, the effects of the Japanese tub routine are quite similar to those of an American cocktail party. At the hour when we try to soothe our frazzled nerves with an ounce or two of alcohol, the Japanese seek, from similar motives, the embrace of hot water. "When I have a worry," a Japanese confided to me, "I make it a rule to go into the tub. I go into it a pessimist and come out an optimist."

A typical Japanese gesture is to provide a brimful tub. Whether it has symbolical meaning or whether the overflow helps to skim impurities from the water's surface, whatever the reason, it is impressive. Newcomers are confused by such lavishness, and some have been known laboriously to ladle out enough water to make room for themselves. Whenever I take a plunge into a full tub, displacing gallons of more or less precious hot water, I cannot help wondering whether Archimedes bathed à la japonaise.

If a brimful tub is an astonishing sight, so much the more are tubs continuously overflowing with scalding-hot water. It is still the stonecutter's business to cut bathtubs from blocks of marble or granite, although their high cost puts them out of reach for ordinary people. Examples of his art are usually found in the bathrooms of inns—single, double, and family-size tubs, miniature pools in the form of a lute, basins hewn into rock. At spas, where bathing goes on at all hours, balneal scenography is limited by the innkeeper's budget only. The principal caldarium of an elegant inn often resembles a watering place for the horses of Valkyries rather than a bathroom: water cascading from great height over gigantic boulders covered with moss and multicolored mineral sediments; a fragmentary pine grove and assorted shrubs; and, even more incongruously, an aquarium with white carp built into one of the walls. Sometimes the splendor of the nymphean retreats is topped by a view—anything from an intimate garden to a sweeping panorama of mountains and islands.

Still more spectacular, if only by virtue of a helping hand from nature, is the Japanese outdoor bath. It is unlike our swimming pools—no diving board, no reef-blue tiles, no chlorinated water. Instead, it is of a bucolic sort—a purling brook amid a glade of trees; a swift flow of steaming water traversing a mountain ravine; a placid lake whose water contains alum, iron, and hypochloric acid, "only needing to be diluted and sweetened in order to constitute an excellent lemonade"[89]; a miniature gorge with arbors and secret nooks, with dressing- and washing-rooms hidden behind rocks. Above all, it is a *hot* pool—sometimes boiling hot. To lie in the water's embrace, the darkness of the night scarcely lessened by a stone lantern or the light of a thin moon, the air resounding with the song of nightingales, is balm for a man who, in a lifetime of bathing, has focused on nothing more stimulating than the sight of a toilet seat and the sound of a flush.

The sociable side of the bath is often vastly more exotic than its mechanics. A couple from God's own country embarking in a matrimonial tub for the first time may feel adventurous and not a little self-conscious. Instead of sipping bourbon and water on their porch, they find themselves seated vis-à-vis in a marble tub shaped to resemble a rowboat, with bow, stern, and two benches. Spankingly

sober, they contemplate each other although, thanks to the haze of hot steam, visibility is benignly poor. Words remain unspoken, thoughts unavowed. Drifting, as it were, through an Oriental Hades in a stony skiff without oars, they never felt so lost. Tomorrow they will ask for separate bathrooms or take their bath in turns.

Whatever the pleasure of company in the bath, most Westerners are unenthusiastic about sharing their bathwater with strangers. Precautions and cleanly habits notwithstanding, companionable bathwater tends to opaqueness, and travelers who patronize country inns far from hot springs make it a rule to arrive early. The inconvenience of cutting short one's journey in the middle of the afternoon

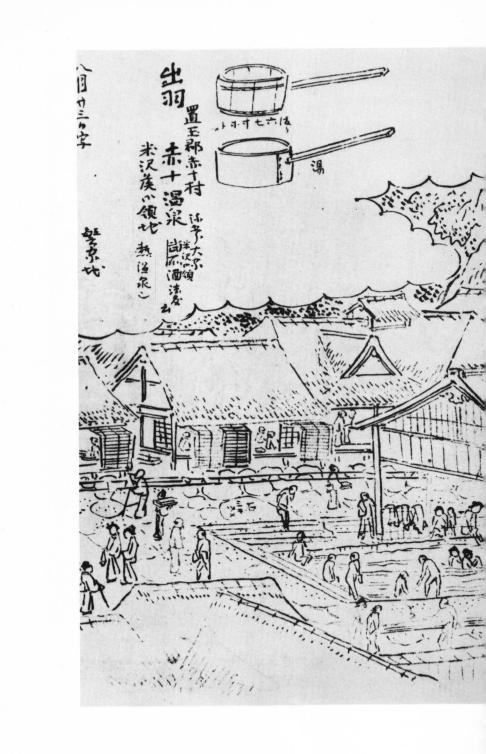

出羽

置玉郡赤十村

赤十温泉

米沢侯ノ領地

八月廿三ノ字

盤京比

湯

（熱温泉）

ife at a popular watering place in the Northern Provinces. Sketched
y Settan Hasegawa.

is compensated for by the prospect of finding immaculate bathwater. Physicians do not object to the custom of sharing a tub as unhygienic. Indeed, compared to the marinade of our swimming pools, Japanese bathwater seems unexceptionable. Provided their bathroom is large enough, a family (which, as a rule, is a small crowd) takes a bath together. In the average household there is likely to be only a small tub, accommodating one person at a time, and it takes all of an evening until everybody has had his turn. Precedence is scrupulously observed. First to mount the tub is the honorable guest. He is succeeded by the master of the house and his sons in the descending order of their age. Next come the female members of the family and, lastly, the servants. In some parts of the country where the old customs are still honored, male servants precede the women of the household. Where fuel is precious, the privilege of the bath is extended to the neighbors; "there is a warm intimacy about the evening chats at the bath which keeps close the relationships between women of three or four neighboring households," writes Embree in his village studies.[90]

One looks in vain for this sort of conviviality in the public baths and the pools of watering places. Barriers of age, status, and sex do not come down with the clothes. If anything, nudity makes them insurmountable. Well-formed and hairless as the bodies of the Japanese are, there is something disconcerting about their porcelain anonymity—a soupçon of sexlessness. Like Raphael's angel faces lolling in sweet indolence on little cloud cushions, the uniformly bland expressions of Japanese faces floating on the steaming waters look disturbingly similar. Sometimes a smile offers a guidepost to identification, disclosing, if only intermittently, a highly individual set of teeth. But smiles are rare, and an acquaintance struck up in the bath is not sanctioned outside.

From the time of Perry down to our days, mixed bathing has been a thorn in the side of alien residents. Having bullied their way into the country by threats and fulminations, their missionary itch kept them forever meddling in their hosts' affairs. In Yokohama, the oldest and strongest outpost of the West, mixed bathing in public bathhouses came to an end in 1862 "by force of public opinion as expressed by the foreigners then resident there" (John Black, *Young Japan*).[91] There was never a question of consulting the native residents' opinion. A few years later the government issued a ban on going naked outdoors, not directed, as one might think, against exhibitionists, but to put an end to walking home from the bath without clothes, a practice that had been equally common in medieval Europe. (After a very hot bath, the blood racing in the body obviates the need for coverings, and the thought of having to put on clothes violates the senses much more than does the sight of nudity.) Still, in order to pacify foreigners, the good citizens of Yokohama covered their red-hot bodies, and coolies chucked their loincloth in favor of more voluminous, if unsuitable garments. "No Japanese ever saw any impropriety in it [the loincloth] until we pointed it out to them," noted Mr. Black with satisfaction.[92]

Not to lose face, the Japanese added The Dirty Mind to their ethics, but, unacquainted as they were with its workings, took little pleasure in it. Their sense of propriety—the nude is seen in Japan but not looked at—coupled with their desire to appear respectable in the eyes of the Western world, brought about one of the situations that are the despair of the militant tourist: in resort towns stalked by missionaries and diplomats, the Japanese have updated their bathing etiquette to meet the most exalted expectations of foreigners, while only a stone's throw from their trails life goes on unregenerate and unspoiled. The real testing grounds of Japan's Westernization in the line of bathing are without doubt the new territories, such as the public beach.

Although the Japanese rear formidable champion swimmers, swimming is not among their ordinary achievements. It is strictly a competitive sport. So little does swimming appeal to them that, according to the *Official Guide,* "during World War II, swimming was almost forgotten."[93] The Welfare Ministry (in a letter to the author) disclosed that 7635 children under the age of fourteen drowned during 1957, a heavy toll in view of their short vacation and even shorter bathing season. An investigation of the wholesale drowning of schoolchildren in a river (while bathing under supervision) brought to light the fact that only one of four instructors could swim.[94]

Boy, indulging in wishful swimming. From *Ancient and Modern Various Usages of Tokio Japan,* 1885.

In Japan a child in peril of drowning is a luckless child. "We feel," writes Lily Abegg in *The Mind of Asia,* "that it is natural to save a drowning child; the East Asian, however, thinks it is unnatural to risk his life if he is not related to the child, which in any case might turn out to be 'only a girl.' "[95] Fortunately, in Japan, beach activities are mostly limited to the national pastimes of sleeping and eating. Swimming is too tiring for men, too masculine a sport for women. Although they all dote on water, they do not think much of getting wet outside of a tub or pool; they leave the rivers and seas to the fish.

There is one exception to the rule. At least once during the summer—traditionally, on the first Sunday in August—townspeople and rural folk go for a picnic to some pretty beach. At T***, on the Shikoku side of the Inland Sea, where I made my home, the beach and the bathing are superb. The shore, hemmed in by a grove of pine trees as old as creation, stretches for about two miles in one perfect curve and although it lies in the path of typhoons, it is well protected by several mountain ranges. Yet T*** is not a resort, hardly a town, at best a fishermen's beach that most of the time looks like a stage set for a ballet. From tall wooden poles hang dragnets dyed baby blue and black, strawberry blond and green—to suit the caprices of fish—with globes of iridescent glass for floaters. In the hot sun, shrimp and sardines are drying on mats and wooden trays, while in the shade of high-pooped boats men, women, and children are sorting the day's catch. No coastal steamers or excursion boats ever enter the bay except on the occasion of the annual beach picnic when the grove is turned into a fair.

On that August Sunday thousands of people arrive by bus and bicycle to camp under the ancient pines. They spread mats and newspapers on the ground, string awnings from the trees and settle down to a rustic meal, washed down with rice-wine and beer. The men strip to their long underwear while the women sport the sketchiest of wrappers—kerchiefs, spidery towels and sashes in picturesque disarray. Half awash in the gentle surf, a few children and their young mothers play in advanced stages of undress. Some are bare to the waist, adding to the scene a touch of the South Seas. A few intrepid souls, immersed to the chin, make motions of swimming with their arms. In their long white slips they recall Bellini's priests diving into the canals of Venice in search of the cross.

Farther out, where the bottom of the bay dips abruptly and large seagoing fishing boats cast anchor, a lone swimmer, a young Japanese woman, is giving proof of her skill. What earned her the envy of the other women (the men pay no attention to the fair sex) is not her swimming style but her bathing suit. It is the color of yellow chrysanthemum, reflecting now and then the glint of a sun already low over the neighboring hills. Only fish keep her company, and, as is their habit at that hour, are cutting capers in the glassy sea, jumping high into the air, in pairs and sometimes in schools.

The lone swimmer seems to be done with the day, and, with a few vigorous strokes, returns to the shore. At the water's edge she looks for the spot where she left her wooden sandals, finds them and slips them on. Then, not without some difficulty—one can easily see that she is not used to it—peels off her bathing suit of fashionable but conservative cut. This done, she throws it over her arm, and, without a wrap, without a stitch, without a trace of self-consciousness, walks away—a living allegory of modern Japan.

Page from a puppet play score printed in the florid *hentaigana* style.

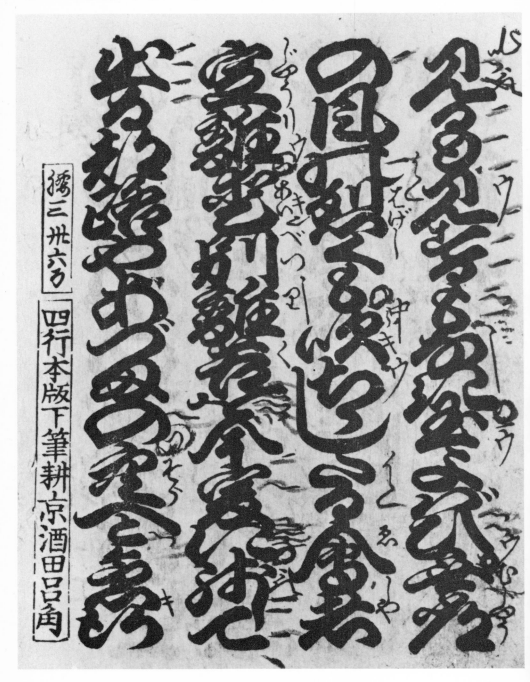

On Language

By merely skimming the English columns in the pages of a Japanese phrase book, one perceives at once the mock-profundity of every utterance. The general lilt of the conversation comes through clearly in the literal translation:

> "Japan-language in, this as-for, what that say?"
> "Plenty inconvenient is."
> "Convenience according!"
> "August convenience if-is-good."
> "That side as-for, convenience good will-probably-be."
> "It differs."

Only unimaginative people conceive of language as a means of communication. Language, said Herbert Spencer, must truly be regarded as a hindrance to thought. At best, languages are tools for obstructing communication. If this sounds paradoxical, remember that they were intended as such by the Lord. Whatever the supposed merits of dubbing and simultaneous-translation earphones, they have not succeeded in defeating His design.

Before the Curse, all the world spoke Babylonian. As every child knows, the Lord confused people's tongues to frustrate a building program that had grown too ambitious, too advanced for its time. Whereas our steepled cathedrals are believed to be pleasing to Him (the spire of the tallest of minsters, that of Ulm, soars to more than five hundred feet), the relatively modest height of the Tower of Babel spelled, unaccountably, blasphemy. Yet, with the greatest of misfortunes often being a blessing in disguise, the shutdown of the enterprise led to the Babylonian separatist movement, which in turn brought about the discovery and subsequent colonization of the Japanese islands by a splinter group.

For thousands of years these basic facts of the Japanese descent and the origin of their language were obscured by a tangle of myths—divine, imperial, and plain bawdy. The first to challenge them was the German physicist Engelbertus Kaempfer who lived and traveled in Japan in the 1690s, and amassed a great store of firsthand knowledge. No less an arbiter than the present-day Japanese government acknowledged Kaempfer's *History of Japan* as "one of the earliest authoritative accounts of the country."[96] His summary description of the nation's beginnings has the ring of truth:

"Not long after the Deluge when the confusion of languages of Babel oblig'd the Babylonians to drop their design of building a Tower of uncommon height, and occasion'd their being dispersed all over the world, when the Greeks, Goths and Slavonians departed for Europe, others to Asia and Africa, others for America, that then the Japanese also set out on their Journey: That in all probability after many years of traveling and many incommodities endur'd, they alighted at this remote part of the World; that, being well pleas'd with the situation and fruitfulness, they resolv'd to chuse it for their abode."[97]

Kaempfer's version of the Japanese nation's birth is a good deal less fanciful than the traditional one which claims divine descent not only for the royal family but for its subjects as well. It also would help to account for some of their peculiarities: their aloofness from all non-Japanese, their legendary endurance of incommodities, their addiction to pilgrimages and travel in general, most of all, their convoluted language. No legend hints at why the Japanese-to-be attracted the supreme wrath of the Deity; why their language emerged singularly tormented. Be that as it may, it redounds to their honor to have borne their cross without flinching. Often on the verge of language reform, they never relented. What is more, they came to love their language. It is their secret strength, but it also could become their undoing. A philologist groping his way through the uncanny subtleties of Japanese texts feels instinctively that the Babylonian curse has not worn off.

Lafcadio Hearn, that demon of a Japan-lover, who renounced two countries for the unglamorous atmosphere of Japanese provincial towns, who changed his English name to a Japanese one, never bothered to learn the language of his adopted country. Although he took a Japanese wife and begot a number of children, he, like many another professional Japan enthusiast, drew the line at the language. "Could you learn all the words in a Japanese dictionary," he wrote, "you would not make yourself understood in speaking unless you learned to think like a Japanese—that is to say, to think backwards, to think upside-down and inside out."[98]

The foreigner coming face to face with the language, be it the spoken or the written word, is pleasantly suffused with the child-like irresponsibility of an Alice in Wonderland. He feels no urge to arm himself with the equivalent

(97) 明 ※ (I—242) ↑	明 明 明 明 1-1-26 (p.55) 明 (stroke order diagram)	**MEI** (abbr. of *Meiji*) **MYŌ** tomorrow **MIN** (*Ming*, a Chinese dynasty) aki(raka) clear; distinct; obvious a(keru) (v.t.) to open; (v.i.) dawn aka(rui) bright; clear; well-versed aka(ri) a light
		明 日 myōnichi; ashita tomorrow akuruhi, the next day (37)
		明 治 Meiji p.n. (era) (565)
		文 明 bummei civilization (240)
(98) 何 ※ (I—88) ↑	何 何 何 何 1-1-27 (p.56) 何 (stroke order diagram)	**KA** nani } what; any nan izu(re) which; either……or; some day izukun(zo) (7) how; however; why
		何 人 nannin, how many poeple nampito who; anyone (30)
		何 分 nanibun anyhow; at all events nampun how many minutes (14)
		如 何 ikan; ikani what manner; how ikaga, how (98)
(99) 入 ※ (I—36) ↑	入 入 入 1-1-27 (p.56) 入 (stroke order diagram)	**NYŪ** **JU** i(ru) (v.i.) to enter; need hai(ru) (v.i.) to enter i(reru) (v.t.) to put in iri entry; income; beginning
		入 口 irikuchi; iriguchi an entrance (109)
		封 入 fūnyū (n.v.) to enclose in (545)
		入 梅 nyūbai the beginning of the rainy season (905)

of those simpering phraseologies known as college French and tourist Italian. The Japanese language looms as a never-never land which few dare to explore. It simply is not a tourist's dish. Moreover, anybody who has acquired by some gruesome brain manipulation the faculty to speak Japanese, realizes how futile were his efforts. His difficulty in communicating with the Japanese has merely grown in depth.

Among the foremost grievances of Westerners is the Japanese distaste for intelligible speech. "To give in so many articulate words one's innermost thoughts and feelings," wrote Inazo Nitobe, "is taken among us as an unmistakable sign that they are neither profound nor very sincere."[99] Far from being uneasy about their obtuseness, the Japanese cultivate it. Only rarely do they hint at their own difficulties. "Verbal expression," said Okakura-Yoshisaburo, another professional explainer and lecturer to Western audiences, "even if there is no intentional mystification on the speaker's part, but, on the contrary, a purpose even explicitly to state his mind as clearly as possible, does not always help the hearer much to the true meaning, unless there has existed from the beginning a certain sympathy between the two, resulting from a similar development in their respective pasts."[100] Paradoxically, such inability to express themselves in articulate speech gives the Japanese a sense of superiority similar to that which the women of Old China derived from their bound feet. Their inability to walk set them apart from the pedestrian mob.

"In the Japanese language exactness of expression is

There are upwards of 80,000 ideograms. A knowledge of 3000 is necessary to read a newspaper. Even the simplest of them permit several interpretations (see right column). Handwriting (see left column) poses problems unimaginable to people who use two dozen letters only.

purposely avoided," says a contemporary writer, Sumié Mishima. "In modern Japanese prose writings of ordinary levels, the reader feels as if he were being led blindfold through a maze with a stick to guide his steps."[101] Hidetoshi Kato, a sociologist, compares the ambiguity of Japanese communication to that of a Rorschach test, "but unlike Rorschach," he says, "there is supposed to be only one correct meaning in the ambiguity."[102] It simply is not among the functions of the Japanese language to elucidate a thought. It only touches on it. Which makes it the ideal medium for their frothy kind of poetry:

> Matsushima!
> Ah! Matsushima, ah!
> Matsushima, ah!

The poem, reproduced in its entirety, is by Bashô (1644–94), if not their most illustrious surely their most beloved and most often quoted poet. The subject is an archipelago in northern Japan—hundreds of islands carved by the sea into fanciful battlements to which cling the tortured shapes of pine trees—a flawless japonaiserie. The subtlety of Bashô's verses puts you off at first, but repeated recitation reveals a vision of unutterable beauty.

In Japan, writing poetry is not the prerogative of maladjusted persons. Poetry parties are no more disreputable than bridge parties. On New Year's Day the entire nation —including the emperor's family—compete for honors at a poetry contest. From all over the world, Japanese and non-Japanese send their melancholy verses. Yet poetry is not confined to aesthetic imagery. Pronouncements that decide the lives of millions of people are sometimes couched in poetic double-talk. "An episode from the war annals," writes Kazuo Kuroda, "has it that the Emperor (Hirohito) tried to express his desire for peace by reciting a poem of his grandfather, the late Emperor Meiji, at the crucial conference where the decision for the Pacific War was made." Explains Mr. Kuroda: "That the Emperor Hirohito in 1941 could not take any stronger measure than mere recitation of that poem is quite understandable to those who know the history of Japan."[103]

In their endeavors to save face, the Japanese are able to climb heights of detachment ordinarily reserved for stage characters only. Nitobe, discoursing on the spirit of daring and bearing, relates the death of Ota Dekan, builder of the castle of Tokyo, a piece of preposterous, if authentic history. When fatally pierced by a spear, "his assassin, knowing the poetical predilection of his victim, accompanied his thrust with the couplet:

> Ah! how in moments like these
> Our heart doth grudge the light of life;

whereupon the expiring hero, not a wit daunted by the mortal wound in his side, added the lines:

> Had not in hours of peace,
> It learned to lightly look at life."[104]

Although quick repartee and ready wit are rarely encountered among today's Japanese, they play a creditable semantic hide-and-seek. They cleansed their language of its functional impurities and elevated it to an abstract art. They have no love for clumsy foreigners who pester them for explanations and elucidations; who dig for a meaning until it stands revealed. Hence the translator is made the whipping boy for all linguistic ills.

Few Japanese are fluent in European languages, and fewer still can translate correctly. Indeed, competent translators are so rare as to form a special caste. Being wordy people, they are apt to let themselves get carried away by their verbal flood and to launch into fabrications of their own. So flagrant is their license sometimes that even a person innocent of any knowledge of Japanese discovers the deceit. Perry, who probably didn't know a word of Japanese, was quick to see through his translator Yenosuke Murayama. "The commodore," reads the official *Narrative,* "did not believe a word of his interpretation, however adroit, and plainly told Yenosuke so. This imputation, though it expressed a doubt of his truthfulness, did not offend the interpreter in the least, but was rather taken as a compliment of his duplicity, which is one of the cherished accomplishments of Japanese officials."[105] Fully three hundred years before Perry, the Jesuit padre Frois expressed the same misgivings: "To tell a lie to a man's face is considered an offense among us; the Japanese laugh it off and take it for urbanity."[106]

Accusations of this sort do not ruffle the composure of a Japanese. He may reply that his thoughts are too subtle for translation; that his rendering them into an uncongenial idiom is an approximation at best. No harm is done, he thinks, if thoughts are left unsaid, or words go untranslated. To him, the intricacies of etiquette are far more important than those of syntax and grammar. Polite speech comes before intelligible speech. Thus, by the time your words have passed through the filter of his mind, their meaning has been lost. Conscientiousness has been supplanted by tact, precision by pomposity. In sum, a Japanese interpreter seems to be under a compulsion to vaporize a thought and to make the most gripping ideas sound innocuous.

It is only fair to mention that the very fogginess of the Japanese language has its good points. It sustains an even temperature of colloquy, discourages confidences, and preserves an all-important standoffishness. The supreme medium of communication is, not surprisingly, silence—a rather sullen silence, indistinguishable from boredom. It never fails to impress Westerners, though. Indeed, it has fostered the belief that all Japanese are philosophers ordained by nature. On closer acquaintance, however, this belief is shattered. Usually silence means that their train of thought has jumped the track.

Their lapidary poetry notwithstanding, the Japanese are anything but short-winded. Where we manage with a simple sentence or two, they are apt to release veritable avalanches of spooky prose. It simply won't do to say that you are leaving early tomorrow and what about the bill. Literally: "Five-hours half, at rousing want-to-obtain, please bill-writing carrying coming condescend." Such condensed guidebook Japanese does not get you anywhere. The complex message has to be chopped up into tiny earfuls, patted and moistened with generous amounts of spittle and kneaded into acoustic pellets to be dispatched one by one with perfect timing. Some of them are bound to miss their target, but you must not despair and keep up the bombardment.

You must do as the Japanese do and take your time with address and rejoinder. Keep in mind that they are unfamiliar with our athletic régime of hardening the eardrums, snatching the thread of discourse from others, drowning words with laughter and expletives, talking fast while trying to follow the conversation of others. Such mental acrobatics are disconcerting to a Japanese who regards speech as vocal ornament rather than a tool. Seeking as he is aesthetic pleasure from the sound waves, he hates nothing more than to be distracted by a verbal message.

Once I sat through a dinner at which twenty-four speeches were made, one by each of the attending guests. Far from delivering them in the boisterous mood that springs from satiety and congenial company, the speakers affected the graceful whisper suitable to the intimacy and

acoustics of a nine-foot-square teahouse. They remained inaudible to any but those sitting close to them. Yet such was their breeding that nobody felt cheated of his share of decibels, nobody shouted "Louder!" The Japanese have a faculty of enjoying speech regardless of content. For all we know, the murmur of digestive oratory sounds delightful to their ears, like softly falling rain or the poetic drip-drip of water from a bamboo pipe.

This makes the Japanese the world's best listeners. Foreign lecturers get along with them famously until they discover that their most brilliant addresses are, in effect, soliloquies. A lady of many years residence in Japan told me of a Frenchman, a disciple of Bergson's, who delivered a series of philosophical lectures in his native language in Tokyo. My informant, erudite though she is, and despite having French as her mother tongue, dropped out of the lectures because they were, she confessed, far above her head. So did a good many of her compatriots. The only ones who remained to the end, unwilling to miss a single word, were Japanese. They would have been surprised at the thought that a knowledge of French was necessary to benefit from the lectures.

"Their art of *seeming* to understand English is perfect," writes an American scholar, Henry C. Bush; "visiting Englishmen and Americans come and talk and leave without guessing that no one in that consummately polite audience understood a whole connected paragraph."[107] Foreigners who see through the pious fraud and are tactless enough to kick up a row, will not ingratiate themselves with their hosts. To the Japanese, the thought that a speaker, celebrated or not, casual or formal, should attach importance to being understood reveals a small mind. Incomprehension on the highest level has its own merits, even when they are not discernible to us. Perhaps we ought to take a leaf out of the Japanese book. Cultural differences or no cultural differences, if we want to get along with the rest of the world, we cannot afford to be dogmatic.

An Appetite for Rice

Unlike most Japanese men, my friend Isamu does not object to being invited to dinner at one's house, if only because his travels abroad made him tolerant of foreign customs. Perhaps I ought to explain that in Japan the way to honor a guest is to take him to a restaurant, less in order to provide for his bodily comforts than to afford him a temporary escape from the engulfing ugliness of modern life. Japanese-style restaurants are often the last holdover from the hallowed past, and to most guests the food they offer is far less important than their soothing atmosphere. Not without good reason did the emperor choose a Tokyo restaurant as the most suitable place for giving his daughter away. Anybody who thinks that, for lack of a Japanese Westminster Chapel, an ancient shrine on a holy mountain would be more appropriate is mistaken. It only goes to show that our tastes and theirs are worlds apart.

One day Isamu let himself be persuaded to dine at my Tokyo apartment and, after he had slowly eaten a lobster bisque, a châteaubriand, and a chocolate mousse, I asked him whether he had liked the food.

It is not his way to blurt out an opinion; a thoughtful man, he takes his time.

"No rice," he finally decided. "A meal without rice is no meal."

He was far from being rude. In fact, he could not have expressed himself more felicitously. The Japanese language itself bears out his point: the word *gohan* stands for both, *a meal* and *boiled rice*. The two are synonymous. Although Japan's waters teem with fish, and her beef is the best in the world, fish and meat are considered little more than accessories to a meal. A Japanese can do perfectly well without either. But he will not forgo his rice.

To a Japanese nothing else tastes as good as rice—Japanese rice, that is, prepared in the native way. Indeed, rice is *the* national delicacy. It is judged for quality and texture with the same sensory attention a Frenchman brings to tasting wine. A Japanese without rice is like a flower without water. Rice is the elixir of life. Rice he must have if he is not to lose his racial identity. He eats, drinks, and dreams rice. Sated, he still craves rice. In Japan, even cats and dogs, if they are lucky, are fed rice. Rice being the measure of all things, for centuries taxes and tributes were paid in rice. Even today, the planting, transplanting, and harvesting of rice is accompanied by religious and secular rites. In the paddies, farmers offer prayers and flowers to the rice god, scatter toasted rice and, in symbolical purification of the fields, pour rice wine onto the good earth.

Although city people think little of the rural rites, they would not dream of missing the gastronomical orgies and human sacrifice associated with them. The apotheosis of rice dishes are *mochi,* cakes made from steamed rice that has been pounded to a paste; they are superlatively indigestible, a hazard to life. The Japanese grow ecstatic about them. To say that they are fond of them is an understatement; they literally give their lives for them.

At New Year's, when the nation is caught in the grip of the *mochi* mystique and the consumption of *mochi* is at its peak, newspapers print culinary casualty lists. According to the *Japan Times* of January 3, 1960 (in more recent years these obituaries have been omitted), in the city of Tokyo

> "about 9 a.m. Mrs. S. M., 53, died of suffocation while being taken to the hospital in Itabashi-ku. She choked after swallowing boiled mochi at the New Year's Day breakfast in her son's home.
> "About 3 p.m. S. N., 66, of Katsushika-ku choked to death after swallowing baked mochi at his home.
> "About 5 p.m. M. M., 55, proprietor of a restaurant in Itabashi-ku, died after he swallowed baked mochi at his home."

And so forth.

On the whole, however, after two thousand years of cultivating and eating rice, the Japanese have superbly adjusted to their diet. Their intestines have grown one foot longer than those of other people, their stomachs have dropped several inches, mainly, as one writer points out, "because of the heavier weight which rice imposes on the stomach."[108]

The ability to prepare rice in the Japanese manner is the touchstone of a woman's competence as a cook. Not only are other systems of cooking rice inacceptable to them, they will eat only the short-grained native variety. In 1861, when the first Japanese goodwill ambassadors set out on a journey to Europe and North America, hundreds of cases of rice were added to their baggage (together with candles, oil wicks, and paper lanterns). "Before our departure," one of them recalled, "the organizers of the embassy had de-

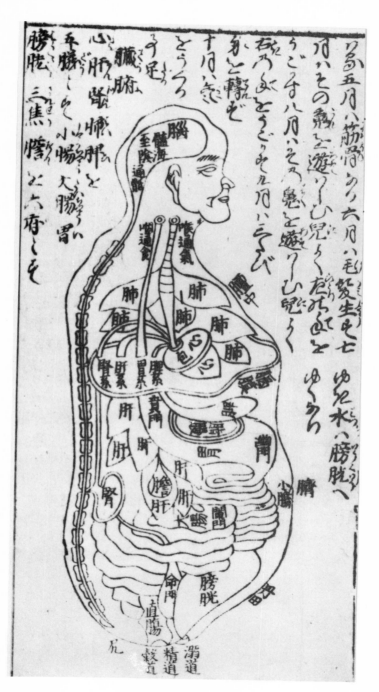

From an eighteenth-century encyclopedia.

cided that we should carry along all the necessary food, because agreeable food would not be available in foreign lands."[109] And so they did. In Paris the party of forty put up in the 600-room Hôtel du Louvre, one of the most luxurious hostelries of the time. The food was famous; its chefs de cuisine ranked in importance with prime ministers, yet their cookery did not gain the confidence of the rice-worshipers. They remained courteously skeptical.

Neither the passage of time nor the inroads of Westernization have changed the Japanese attitude to foreign food. Even residence abroad does not affect their tastes. I have known Japanese, fully endowed with the sensibility so readily associated with their race, who lived in France for years, exposed to her dishes and wines, and never retained so much as the aftertaste of a gastronomical memory. Their culinary experience does not harden into knowledge.

But then, most Americans abroad act and react much the same. Those who distrust the national dishes of Europe find their idiosyncrasies fearfully magnified in Japan. "Among the refreshments served to me were *living fish*," wrote Townsend Harris with alarm.[110] (His italics.) Without doubt, he meant to say *raw fish;* he probably panicked at his first sight of *sashimi*. Men of stronger gustatory nerves are known to have made peace with Japanese food unconditionally. After some initial difficulties with the Japanese diet, Edward Morse proudly noted in his diary: "I had for supper marine worms—actual worms, resembling our angleworms, only slightly larger. . . . They were eaten raw and the taste was precisely as seaweed smells at low tide. I ate a large plateful and slept soundly."[111] A marine biologist, he probably could not help being in their favor.

Guidebooks never fail to caution the tourist against what they take to be the hidden dangers of Japanese food ("to

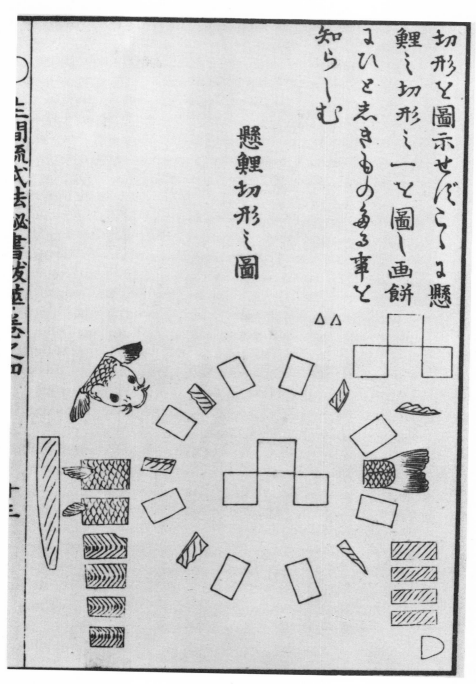

切形と圖示せらゝゝま懸
鯉ゝ切形ゝ一と圖し画餅
よひと志きものゝ有る事と
知らしむ

懸鯉切形ゝ圖

Diagram showing how to cut a carp for *sashimi*. From an etiquette book.

raw fish cholera is traceable"[112]) and give advice on how to make it edible—"by adding salt and sugar to the always obtainable rice, and pouring milk over it, a palatable substitute for porridge is obtained."[113] They never say how to revive one's Japanese dinner companions from their dead faint over such culinary sacrilege. A Japanese would rather starve than eat the monstrosity. Muragaki, the first Vice Ambassador to the United States (in 1861) reported that the embassy staff arrived at Philadelphia "very hungry as we had only had a few slices of bread in the morning. The manager of the hotel knew that we liked rice and proudly served it; but, how wonderful was the way in which it was cooked! Fried in butter!! Butter is a form of diet to which we are unaccustomed and our stomachs refuse to accept it. So we politely requested that this dish should be removed. The next course, to our renewed disappointment, was rice cooked with sugar! We finally gave up all hope of rice and turned to bread to appease our appetites."[114] Thus, food stands, a major obstacle, in the way of appreciating other cultures. Not counting the many who are indifferent to food in general, one can match every enthusiast with an objector.

To many Americans the very thought of Japanese food is unnerving. Food phobias and fears flare up violently, causing them to lose their appetite as well as their temper. Perry's officers partaking of a sumptuous Japanese state dinner thought to detect "flavor of cat, dog, rat and snake,"[115] if only because most of them never had tasted anything more exotic than Boston beans. "The entertainment of the Japanese," remarked Perry, "left an unfavorable impression of their skill in cookery."[116] But so probably would the skill of European cooks. The proof of the pudding is not always in the eating, for many a palate is unreceptive to food that lies outside its experience. Perry's

A row of rice cookers in an opulent kitchen. From an etiquette book for women, 1660.

men smelling a rat in their welcome dinner reflects less on Japanese cooking than on their culinary intolerance.

Japan and the West differ considerably in their approach to food preparation. The best of European cooking is a kind of culinary alchemy—the transformation of edible substance into a gastronomical work of art. A good cook does not depend on either rare or costly victuals. On the contrary, his greatest pride often lies in his ability to produce a good meal with humble ingredients. A measure of ingenuity and enterprise, a knack for improvisation, outweigh a lifetime's stolid routine.

Almost none of this applies to Japan. Japanese cooks never extemporize. Unadventurous by temperament, they simply would not dream of concocting new dishes or tampering with traditional ones. They never bring forth a Carême or an Escoffier. Their cooking is as automatic as flying by instruments. Indeed, so much so that whereas the most expert practitioner of Western cooking follows the progress of his work by frequent tasting, a Japanese cook may never have sampled the better part of his stock-in-trade. He works by rote and considers tasting vulgar.

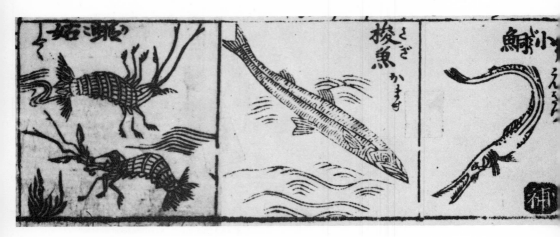

Luckily, most Japanese cooking is instant cooking—no stews simmering for eight hours in sealed casseroles, no pâtés and sauces concocted from secret recipes. Kitchen chemistry is reduced to a minimum. Since, however, the components and preparation of a dish rarely vary, the result suffers; the gratifying immediacy of the first experience fades with repetition.

The gastronomical monotony is perhaps felt more acutely because rice wine is served with *every* dish. According to Japanese notions, there isn't a dish—rice excepted—with which *sake* cannot be drunk. Yet, non-Japanese remain unconvinced. Half of the pleasure of a civilized Western meal depends on the choice of wine, or wines, and although *sake,* whose flavor comes nearest to sherry, goes well with any number of soups, to pretend that one enjoys it with every kind of fish or meat is to carry politeness too far. Nevertheless, it is exactly its sweetness which makes *sake* so satisfactory to the Japanese. In their book sweetness and excellence are the same, just as red and beautiful are synonymous to the Russians.

Instead of swapping culinary know-how with other na-

Lobster, pike, eels. From a seventeenth-century encyclopedia.

tions, the Japanese continue in their old ways. They are far more at pains to preserve their singular talent for making every meal an aesthetic experience. To say that an elegant Japanese dinner is a lesson on how to eat with one's eyes is not an empty cliché. As a matter of fact, on supreme occasions such as imperial banquets, as we have already mentioned, court etiquette demands that the guests be content with *looking* at the food.

Maybe there was a time, now forgotten, when contemplation of food was all there was to a meal; when tumescence of the gastric juices achieved much the same purpose as does our laborious biting, chewing, and swallowing. For thousands of years human inventiveness has been at work to make the business of stoking our stomachs less humiliating, yet neither fasts nor fads permit us to forget that, by our body functions, we are animals, pure and simple. I sometimes ask myself whether we have not misread the Bible; whether the original curse inflicted on mankind was not Food.

No menus are extant from the time of the Fall, but the great ado about the apple suggests that up to the notorious incident the practice of eating was unknown to man. He led, it would seem, a semiangelic existence, blessedly unaware of his digestive tract, the trickiness of its workings, and the general unsavoriness of metabolism. Only after yielding to his desire to eat did he fall, evolutionally speaking, from the state of grace to the status of homo sapiens, committing himself to a lifelong struggle with hunger and thirst, with obesity, inebriety, and the attendant gastroenterological disorders. All our efforts to mitigate the curse of a food-conditioned existence did not restore us to an approximation of angelhood. What we got instead are wonder diets and laxatives, maîtres d'hôtel and Musak. The people who have come closest to purging eating of its brutishness are the Japanese. Their achievement lies less in their cooking skill than in their manipulation of food. It is the mechanics of ingestion that they have perfected to an art unknown to other people.

If Isamu knew that he had made a gaffe, he did not betray his feelings. Western food, he said without regret, did not agree with him. I remembered that he had been hospitalized on account of stomach trouble, and, seeing my chance to get off the subject of food, I asked him to tell me about his experience. Alas, after some words of praise for his doctors and nurses, he went right back to food—hospital food. Or rather, he told of his grievance with the manner in which it was served. "It is depressing to eat from white dishes," he said, avoiding looking at the table in front of him. To sidestep the issue, he recited a poem by Jûgaya:

> A European meal;
> Every blessed plate and dish
> Is round.

Surely anyone brought up in a well-appointed old-style Japanese house is struck by the sickroom, indeed, the operating-room quality, of our table settings—the shrouded table, the asceptic look of the dinnerware, the variety of surgical instruments for dissecting and paring, for cutting a sinew or laying bare a bone. Floral offerings and lighted candles, far from enhancing the food, shift the mood from the convalescent stage to the lying-in-state. Our custom of lighting candles for our live dinner guests is disturbing to a Japanese.

The profusion of shapes and materials of Japanese dinnerware, the variety of glazes and tints, are bewildering at first. Plates are square, triangular, and polygonal, or shaped to resemble leaves or fans. Cups and bowls imitate

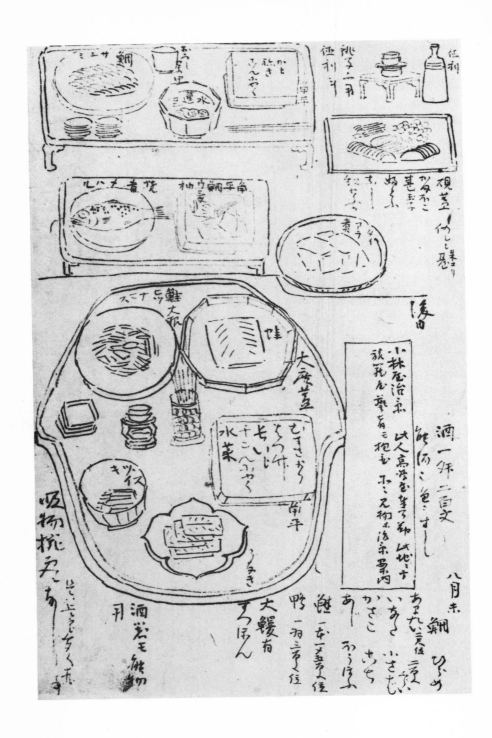

folded paper, seashells, fish of known and imagined species. Since every container has a specific function, the choice of bowls, cups, and trays automatically determines what goes into them. The Japanese dislike of matching pieces results in a surfeit of aesthetic promiscuity, but somehow this exuberance is not jarring. The austerity of a Japanese room, rather than setting off the burst of color, has an attenuating effect on it.

Each dish is in itself a crisp composition. "Raw fish," for instance, belies the crudity it implies in English—several morsels of rosy tuna, a few alabaster slices of cuttlefish, the sprig of an herb, a curl of seaweed, a tiny chrysanthemum blossom, are fitted neatly into place. The sauce into which the fish is dipped comes in a separate bowl. Not a drop of it mars the still life. Compare this arrangement to what we call a "serving" and you will understand why the Western custom of heaping food, however gingerly, onto a single plate is revolting to the Japanese. Nothing could be less appetizing to them than the Ur-chaos of turkey meat, whipped potatoes, vegetables, gravy, stuffing, and cranberry jelly that to us spells festive fare.

Whereas we set a table with empty plates, the Japanese lay out the complete meal before anybody is seated. All dishes make their appearance simultaneously. There is no

A traditional, rather elaborate meal at the height of summer. On the uppermost tray: a platter of raw fish; an octagonal bowl with water lotus; a jar with dressing; a square box with noodles. Below the *sake* bottle and cups, a small tray with egg- and fish-cakes and baked soy bean curd. Next row, red snappers prepared in three different ways: broiled, boiled with lemon, and, on the round dish, cooked in sesame oil. On the largest tray, clockwise: salmon in decagonal dish; water vegetables in square container; broiled eel in leaf-shaped dish; appetizers in bowl, and, lastly, giant radish on round dish. Drawing by Settan Hasegawa.

build-up from oysters over fish and game to a climactic roast, no decrescendo over cheese, fruit, and sweet. The meal begins and ends on a note of culinary togetherness. Soup, meat, fish, et al. are served at the same time. More exactly, the food precedes the eater. When he sits down at the table, it has been waiting for him; hot dishes getting cold, cold ones getting warm, achieving uniform tepidity. No matter; "it has been hot once and that suffices," observed Lady Sansom with the awesome tact of a diplomat's wife.[117]

To foreigners who grumble over their frigid fried eggs (whose greasiness adds to the difficulty of picking them up with wooden sticks), the Japanese turn a deaf ear. Conversation that threatens to turn unpleasant is shunned. Cold food, or rather warm food gone cold, has long been taken for granted by them. Since a Japanese kitchen is a far cry from what *we* call a kitchen, it is not unusual for a housewife to cook a full-course dinner on a single burner. By the time she has finished preparations, her meal has heaved the last sigh of warmth. And such are the logistics of an inn that, for all its modern kitchen equipment, the chances of getting anything hot to the table are poor. More often than not, the kitchen is in some remote part of the establishment, the distance sometimes the length of a block, the many corridors wide open to the winds. Hot plates are unknown. Pantries, if any, are used for storage only. No wonder, foreigners find the relatively artless hot dishes of popular cooking, *sukiyaki* and *tempura,* much more to their liking. Perhaps because the first is of humble origin—a dish invented by peasants—and the second was introduced by the Portuguese, they are served without fuss. Both are prepared directly in front of the guest.

On second thought, who can tell whether the Japanese, unbeknown to themselves, do not reveal some extraordinary intuition in their acceptance of tepid food. Why indeed should man eat things hot? The lion who dines on cold cuts is teeming with health, and does not a cat owe its glossy fur and general lissomeness to *tepid* milk? Two questions deserve consideration: Did man have stomach ulcers in that distant past before he learned to build a fire? Was not the mixing of fire and food a hideous mistake?

Be that as it may, a Japanese meal has compensations aside from and in addition to its indisputable culinary delights. When it comes to eating a meal, the Japanese is an uncompromising aesthete. A self-respecting man does not consider a meal a meal, be it only rice, pickles, and tea, unless it is served in style. No raiding the icebox, no guzzling from bottles, no eating from cardboard plates. He likes to sit down and be served by a competent, well-dressed woman.

At an inn, or a restaurant (the genuine article), even at your host's house, a bath is not only available on the premises but more or less de rigueur. As we have noted, the preprandial bath takes the place of our apéritifs and cocktails. It stimulates the appetite without numbing the taste buds or burdening the liver. On every count, the custom is healthier than ours. Even from the point of view of sociability it is superior—convivial immersion in water (under the host's roof, that is—not in a public bath) forms a far stronger bond with one's dinner companions than do the swaths of cigaret smoke at a cocktail party.

The free perspiration of friendliness is encouraged by banishing Western clothes from the table. Strictly speaking, they are not admitted to any honest-to-goodness Japanese house because they are unclean, actually and metaphorically. Don't argue. Your suit, even though it may have come back from the cleaners only today, isn't considered any cleaner than one that reeks of wear. The management or

179

Decorum and domesticity characterized the old-fashioned houses of pleasure. Since their abolition in 1955, a profligate life has to be pursued along Western lines.

your host will provide you with a freshly laundered *Japanese* robe.

To be sure, such a robe does not meet our demands of propriety. Loose coverings at the dinner table smack of orgies. In our book, looseness stands for dissoluteness. Our idea of having a good time is to wear "formal" clothes of studied inconvenience—shirt-front, cuffs, collar, tie, suspenders, garters—the detachable attributes of Western masculinity. We never stop doing penance for our sins. At an elegant dinner, we are still choking, as it were, on Eve's apple.

The Japanese approach to dinner dress is far more subtle than ours. Above all, a Japanese distinguishes clearly between visual and tactile satisfaction from clothes, and experience has taught him that the two are mutually exclusive. As happens so often, his dazzling egotism shows the way out of the dilemma. His solution befits a genius. It is one more example of his gift for having his cake and eating it too: far from being indifferent to dinner clothes, he is a stickler for sartorial correctness; he just happens to project his ideals of being well dressed onto the *other* sex. Thus, while he enjoys his dinner agreeably unbuttoned (figuratively speaking; there are no buttons in Japanese dress), the sight of a woman tightly bound into her kimono gives him aesthetic enjoyment. In his opinion, uncomfortable clothes should be seen but not worn.

A foreigner would do well to acquire at least an elementary knowledge of native table manners. Mere acquaintance with the rules will not suffice for him to make the grade; practice is imperative. Even if he had an open manual of dining etiquette in front of him, it is doubtful that he would conduct himself with any degree of success. He may find that to eat his way through food laid out on *three* tables (that is, three tables for each guest) is as absorbing a task as playing a five-keyboard organ. For make no mistake about it—a Japanese meal is no smörgåsboard. It would be boorish to let yourself be guided by your appetite or fancy.

For the benefit of foreigners the World Fellowship Committee of the Y.W.C.A. of Tokyo has compiled a guidebook to the intricacies of everyday etiquette, or what they call with exemplary tact "the delicate differences between Eastern and Western manners."[118] Elementary dining behavior is discussed in the chapter on Ordinary Meals: "Because rice is considered the principal food," explain the authors of the manual with the patience of a good-natured nurse, "first of all, remove the cover of your individual rice bowl, which is still empty. Since the bowl is always placed on the left-hand side, take off the cover with your left hand and place it at your left facing upwards. Then with your right hand take off the cover of the soup bowl which is at your right and place it to your right . . . you must remember to do these two things in this order at the very beginning of the meal.

"When the rice is to be served to you, take up the empty bowl at your place and, preferably with both hands, set the bowl on the tray extended to you. It is permissible to use only one hand if, for instance, your kimono sleeve is in the way, in which case you hold your right sleeve with your left hand and present your bowl with the right.[119]

"Next, after you have received from the server the rice bowl now filled with rice, you must always remember to place the bowl back upon the table or on your individual tray, for it is very bad form to begin eating the rice without doing this. Only after the rice bowl is placed on the tray or table are the chopsticks taken up in the right hand and arranged with the left ready to be used. Then the rice bowl is taken up with the left hand and one or two mouthfuls of rice are eaten . . ."

If you haven't lost your way—or appetite—by then, "put down your bowl, and with the right hand take up the soup bowl and put it on the palm of the left hand. Some of the soup is drunk first, then some of the contents eaten. Next, rice is eaten again, and then more soup or some other dish on the right-hand side . . ."[120] Like Pavlov's dogs, the hungry eater must earn his food by accurately traversing the maze of table etiquette.

All the above refers to strategy only. A rattail of rules concern policy. "Don't linger over the dishes undecided as to what to eat next. Don't take food from dishes on the farther side without lifting up the dishes. Don't take up dishes on the right side with the left hand or those on the left with the right."[121] Whereas sleeping is pursued doggedly, almost fiercely, eating is characterized by a certain abstractedness, due no doubt to the relative skimpiness of most meals. As it is, one's table companions *do* linger over the dishes. They rove and roam about the food, and when it comes to eating it, nibble as daintily as a bee. Yet even a bee is methodical, cleaning out the honey assets of one blossom before turning to the next, while Japanese etiquette demands that *all* dishes be given equal attention. With luck, the fumbling foreigner gets, literally, a helping hand from unexpected quarters. Invariably a maid or a female member of the host's family is just waiting for her chance to play the guardian angel. She is part of the arrangement; a dinner party often is composed in equal numbers of active and what one might call corresponding members. In other words there are dinner companions who eat and others who don't. Americans learned about this custom on their first contact with Japan. Some notables who had boarded Perry's ship accepted without much ado an invitation to dinner, but when asked to bring their ladies they balked. As Perry noted, they jeered at the very thought of it as "a very amusing but quite impractical joke."[122]

The purported changes of a Japanese woman's position in the past hundred years have not affected domestic protocol. Women rate no higher than condiments at the dinner table. Their lot is to sing, play, dance, serve, and between-whiles bolster the ego of their masters with flirtatious banter. Although most of their stylized charm eludes the Westerner, they will earn his gratitude by helping him negotiate the obstacles of dinner conversation. Ideally suited to play the Good Samaritan, women help a straggler through a meal and nurse any wounds inflicted on his self-respect. Their chief task vis-à-vis a newly arrived foreigner is to teach him how to eat with the wooden sticks.

Japanese convey food to the mouth with that exquisite tool known to us by the inappropriate term of chopsticks (which is pidgin for the heavy Chinese variety). Japanese eating sticks, called *hashi,* are of featherweight wood and not much longer than a pencil. Edward Morse considered them "the most simple and economical device ever invented by man" and earnestly called for their adoption by every one of our public institutions, yet he knew his Americans well enough not to plead the general use of *hashi.* Still, it is a strange comment on our civilization that we need a veritable arsenal of tools to eat our way through a full-course dinner—oyster forks, fish forks, meat forks, forks for fruit and cheese, and about as many knives, plus several spoons. All these have to be cleaned, polished and stored whereas *hashi* are simply thrown away after use.

To most Orientals the idea of attacking a plateful of food with heavy metal instruments is as absurd as chopping parsley with a guillotine. They like to have their food served ready to eat, and prefer to pick it up with their wooden pincers. Aesthetic and economic considerations apart, when it comes to physiological taste, *hashi* are supreme. For whether you are aware of it or not, our table hardware has a disagreeable taste. If you don't notice it, rejoice; your taste buds have been mercifully blunted ever since you were presented with the proverbial silver spoon. Perhaps though, when a piece of tinfoil gets into your mouth while eating cheese, you may perceive its nauseating sweetness. Yet the taste of tinfoil differs from that of other metals only in degree. The fact that most of us are used to the metallic tinge of cutlery does not do away with its unpleasantness for more discerning people. Spicy foods tend to cover it up, and it is the blandness of Japanese food more than anything else that makes *hashi* indispensable.

And yet, for all its Oriental refinements, dining à la japonaise leaves many a Westerner disappointed. It lacks the sensuousness he associates with good eating. Despite his rapture over the exquisite vessels and victuals, the languid motions of diners and cupbearers, he becomes engulfed by a growing exasperation. He remains expectant and probing, as if listening to the tuning of an orchestra with never a sound of music coming forth. He cannot help thinking that a Japanese dinner reaches its climax right at the beginning when the eye takes in the sweep of offerings.

When a dinner nears its end, when there has been enough *sake* drinking and teasing of the palate, a halt is called to frivolity and everybody clamors for rice. (For a Japanese it is taboo to eat rice while drinking alcohol.) As soon as the rice bucket is brought to the room, the guests become hushed and attentive. There is an inaudible sniffing, like a tiger having caught the scent of his prey. Forgotten are self-restraint and grace. At their last chance for filling their stomachs, everybody becomes frantic and with ravenous appetite downs one bowl of the white manna after another.

In former centuries, eating rice was a jealously guarded privilege. In mountain districts where rice was scarce, only the head of a household might eat it. All other family members had to get along with coarse gruel. When the time came for the old man to retire, his privilege was transferred to the eldest son, and, until the end of his days, he had to eat gruel with the others. Well off today, the Japanese are able to indulge in their favorite food to their hearts' content; for the first time in history, they are producing all the rice they can eat.

Affluence tends to imperil a nation's integrity. Today, all over Japan, thousands of restaurants offer foreign dishes, plain and fancy, and although risotto, pilaf, paella, and riz au lait do not appeal to the native palate, they are consumed in quantity. Compared to authentic Japanese dishes ordered in an authentic Japanese restaurant, they are cheap if only because the way one goes about eating a foreign meal is perfunctory. It is gobbled up without ceremony to the sounds of metal on china among an uncongenial crowd—a cheerless affair. The Japanese impart to it a varnish of legitimacy by including rice, whatever the nature of the other courses. Masters of compromise that they are, they have acquired the habit of eating any and every foreign dish—even a rice dish—with generous portions of their own immaculate unseasoned rice on the side. There is no need to order it; it is served as a matter of course and pièce de résistance. It takes the place of our bread. Asked whether they enjoy Western food, they will say that they don't mind it.

In the years after the Pacific War, Western eating habits were introduced not so much by way of etiquette books as through live demonstrations by the foreign soldiery and

their resident dependents. Most of the victors have left
long ago, but their manners and mannerisms are being
faithfully emulated with results such as these: the foreign
visitor who does not relish a native breakfast, if ever so
temptingly served—rice, thick soup, bean curd, seaweed
and coarse tea—and orders a Western one instead, is happy
to see it presented in authentic home fashion. Proud of her
savoir-faire, the maid will serve the food in its original
packaging instead of in the usual porcelain containers—
cereals in their cardboard boxes imprinted with breakfast
epics; condensed milk in a viciously crimped tin can; jam
in a glass jar (in a traditional table setting, glassware is
taboo) and, as the final touch, a bottle of ketchup for painting the eggs red. Whereas native condiments are brought
to the table separately in little bowls, machine-made
American-style sauces are simply slapped on the food by
the cook.

There was a time when Western food and Western
table manners were downright revolting to the Japanese.
Abstinence from meat was firmly rooted in both ritualistic
tradition and innate revulsion, and the idea of eating meat
never occurred to them. Indeed, during the long period of
Japan's seclusion, meat was thought unfit for human consumption. Buddhist injunctions against eating meat had

Marsh mushrooms (opposite page), giant white radish and miniature eggplant are Japanese specialties.

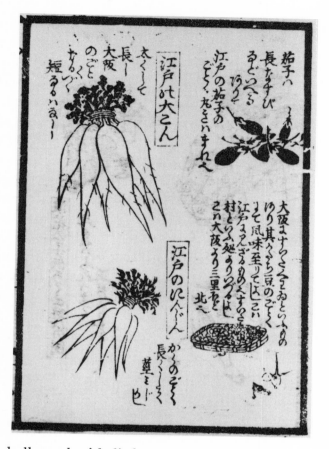

been challenged with little success by Christian missionaries, and although game and fowl were abundant in earlier times, they were forever left in peace. What probably also tilted Japanese taste toward a vegetarian diet is the fact that eating animal fat produces butyric acid which gives the carnivore a disagreeable smell. The Japanese have—or had—a nose for it whereas we, apparently, have not. No more than we have an ear for a dog whistle. "To a Japanese," writes Ichiro Kawasaki (*The Japanese Are Like That*), "Westerners have a strong body odor which is quite nauseating. The body odor of the average American or

Englishman is undoubtedly the result of a heavy meat diet. We find it most curious to read advertisements in Western papers and magazines about lotions and medicines, the use of which will prevent the wrecking of romances and will enhance the user's happiness."[123] The foreigner who seeks romance in Japan may take comfort in the knowlege that he can make himself more attractive by sticking to native dishes. He, too, may thus be able to achieve that exquisite state of being no more fragrant than a lily.

Although Japan never had any holy cows, killing a cow for food was unthinkable. As the Portuguese Jesuit Luis Frois, a sixteenth-century resident of Japan, put it, "we are horrified at the killing of human beings but don't mind killing cows or chickens; the Japanese are horrified at

Book illustration, 1760.

seeing animals killed whereas killing people with them is common usage."[124] The slaughter of cattle was a crime, supposed to invite misfortune upon the community. In his autobiography, Katayama Sen reminiscing about the family ox, says "we loved him as one of ourselves."[125] Seconded historian Shibusawa: "People who had cows and oxen regarded them virtually as members of the family."[126] The first cow to be killed for food with impunity became a national martyr and, since she died to gratify the cravings of an American, it is perhaps in order to unearth the bare bones of her history.

About half a day's travel from Tokyo, at the southern end of Izu Peninsula, lies Shimoda, a small fishing town with little to recommend it. It does, however, a good tourist business on account of its historical associations. Perry landed here in 1854 on his second expedition to Japan, which event is commemorated by an annual Black Ship Festival. In the nearby village of Hamasaki, the first American consul, Townsend Harris, spent the better part of two years while waiting to be recognized by the ruler of Japan. (The temple in which he lived—now as then, temples double as lodging houses for strangers—is being preserved as a memorial.) Harris had been eager for his commission, but when the excitement over the new surroundings had worn off, when his dealings with the authorities seemed to drag on forever, he succumbed to boredom and self-pity. Like many another involuntary hermit, he sought consolation in fleshpots.

A well-traveled and portly man, he was greatly interested in keeping a good table. In a letter to a friend, written shortly after his arrival in Shimoda, he tells of his epicurean diversions. "I am now supplied with wild Boars flesh, which animal abounds in the Hills. The flesh . . . is very tender, juicy, and of an excellent flavor; the taste is between deli-

The harbor and town of Shimoda. From a Japanese scroll, ca. 1810.

cate veal, and the tenderloin of pork;—I am promised a supply of it during the Winter season; in addition to this, I am occasionally furnished with some delicate Venison; fine large Hares, and Golden Pheasants equal to any in the world."[127]

A good American, he felt uneasy about mentioning what at home were regarded as hedonistic tastes. "It seems impertinent to note such small affairs," he apologized in the same letter, "but you must bear in mind that the only animal food used by the Japanese are Fish and Poultry. There is not a sheep or Goat in all Nippon, and the few Bullocks that are kept are used for burden or the plough only; they are never eaten." Near his kitchen he installed a pigpen and a poultry house, yet, two years later, he was down and out, gastronomically speaking. "I am out of flour, butter, lard, hams, bacon, and in fact of all articles of Foreign production, and am reduced to the Japanese diet of Rice and fish."[128]

One of the brighter moments in this monotonous period of his life was the day when beef made its first appearance on his dinner table. The true significance of the occasion seems to have escaped him altogether since he did not mention it in his diary, or, quite likely, remorse and a bad conscience prevented him from writing about it. For the Japanese, however, the event made history. In the temple yard, across from the stone that commemorates the raising of the first American flag on Japanese soil, stands another memorial which reads:

THIS MONUMENT, ERECTED BY THE
BUTCHERS OF TOKYO IN 1931, MARKS
THE SPOT ON WHICH THE
FIRST COW IN JAPAN WAS
SLAUGHTERED FOR HUMAN CONSUMPTION
(EATEN BY HARRIS AND HEUSKEN)

The date of the execution is not given. No flowers grace the epitaph, no incense signals its presence. But then, this is not a grave; the cow ended up in the stomachs of the consul and his secretary. Unfortunately nothing is known about the culinary side of the event. An eight-volume diary written by the elders of the village whose duty it was to spy on Harris may or may not contain some information on the ill-fated beast. As the mayor of Shimoda admits, there is not a soul in town who can read the diary. The reputed high literacy of the Japanese being what it is, a one-hundred-year-old text is to all practical purposes unintelligible to any but an expert linguist. The diary, two silver dollars, two of Harris' cigars, and a chipped wineglass constitute the temple's cultural exhibits. My correspondence with various scholars, with the Tokyo Metropolitan Government and the President of the Meat Wholesalers' Association (who was the instigator and fund-raiser for the bovine monument) shed no light on the more intimate circumstances of the event.

Not until the emperor himself partook of beef—in 1872, about sixteen years after the Shimoda bloodshed in the cause of gluttony—did the meat situation change. As it is, the august culinary coup d'état entailed a miraculous veering around of the national palate—it turned the Japanese age-old horror of meat into a yearning. Whereupon the nation went about promoting the consumption of beef with all the religious zeal that springs from every one of their about-faces. Meat restaurants opened in all big towns, and the authorities hastened to make known the nutritive as well as the prestige values of meat. As one Japanese historian put it, "beef-eating was regarded as a sign of advanced state of civilization."[129] If beef-eating was the price of admission to the Western world, then eating beef was the thing to do. What readjustment the olfactory organ had to undergo was never mentioned.

By then enmeshed in a double self-conceit, the Japanese realized that this was not by far the end of their concessions to foreign ways. If they wanted to eat Western food, they had to have knives and forks which most of them knew from pictures only. To the Japanese, the thought of having to toil at the table, to complete what work the cook had left unfinished, was most unattractive. To chop off bits from a chunk of meat and to impale them on the tines of a fork seemed to them as outlandish as the taste of metal itself. Nevertheless, in the tug of war that ensued between loyalty to tradition and love for up-to-dateness, the latter won out.

If Japan's Western-style cuisine is gastronomically unexciting, their ways of *eating* Western food are often highly original. For example, in the dining car of a train (where the food is Western-style only), Japanese passengers may order lunch at nine o'clock in the morning. Or, they may begin a Western meal with large portions of ice cream as appetizer. Once, sharing a table with a Japanese, I had occasion to admire the resourcefulness of his race. Apparently being no more familiar with Western food and the method for eating it than a Westerner would be at his first visit to a Japanese restaurant, he was examining the table suspiciously when his attention was caught by a pyramid of butter balls on a small plate. For a moment he eyed them speculatively, then pulled the plate nearer to him and, with his *hashi* (he had brought along his own dainty set in a small case), picked up the pellets at a conjurer's speed and hurled them into his mouth.

On the whole the Japanese do not have much opportunity to acquire Western table manners at home. Some of them may hear about the use of cutlery in school where a single lesson is devoted to the abstruse subject. This extracurricular lecture is delivered right in the classroom. At his

A la' Carte　　　　　　一 品 料 理

Consomme Exrvel … … … …	チーズ玉子入スープ … … … … …	¥100
Spaghetti Plogaise	スパゲツチポロゲーズ… … … … …	200
(レバー、小海老、シャンピニオン入　バタソテー、マデラソース)		
Oyster Cremed Minestora or Consomme or Tomato Juice		
カキのヤサイクリームスープ又はコンソメ(温)トマトジュース		100
Brochette de Oysters Anglaise …	カキの銀串刺パン粉焼　マツタケライス添 …	250
Cold Salad de Mexican Fujiya Style	メキシカンサラダ　不二家風	170
Chicken Picata Riest Milanise …	若鶏チーズ玉子包焼　ミラノ風… …	250
Minched Meat Cutlet … … … …	ミンチカツレツ、トルコ　ライス添 …	230
Spaghetti American or Meat Boll …	スパゲツチ 小海老入フライエツグ添 又はミートボール	180
Mignon de Pork Fujiya Style …	豚ヘレ肉　一口カツレツ　不二家風 …	270
Hamburg Switzer Steak … … …	ハンバークステーキ　スイス風 …	170
Pork Chop Ham Maderie … … …	ポークチヤツプ　ハムマデラ… …	250
Panache Monarisa… … … …	小海老と栗リンゴ入新鮮ヤサイサラダ盛合せ…	200
Veal Picata & Beignet de Fish		
小牛の玉子チーズ焼きと鮮魚の衣揚げ	… …	200
Croquette de Shrimps Monte-Curlo	小海老コロツケ　モンテカルロ風	
Vienna Sousage Frast Caustine… …	ウインナソーセージとスパゲツティーバター炒り (フライエツグ添)	170
Pyramid Piraff au Carmerita …	若鶏の身クリーム煮込合せ　ピラミツドライス添 …	220
Veal de Pizza Steak Hapatiain …	犢腿肉ステーキ　パイ包みチーズ焼き … …	230

With no charge of Salad, and Boiled Rice or Bread above dishes.

上記の御料理にはサラダとライス又はパンが付いて居ります

A sampling of Western dishes from a 1960 bill of fare (¥100=28¢). English-language menus often list such mysterious foods as "soft milk" and "pocket cheese." *Coffee olé,* on the other hand, is not a racy Spanish concoction but old-fashioned café au lait.

desk, the teacher officiates at his own meal and, between mouthfuls, comments on the technical subtleties and general philosophy of foreign *etiketto*. Such an extraordinary spectacle cannot, I think, but bruise native sensibility and probably leaves in the audience the same feeling of dejection and embarrassment that I experienced in my youth when a physician was produced in class to inform us, if ever so spuriously, on the facts of life.

In neither case are the pupils expected to put their newly acquired knowledge to the test at once. The actual feat of wielding knife and fork has to wait, for in Japan school lunches are still of the old-fashioned kind. Even the teacher brings his own lunch box of rice and eating sticks along. The occasion to translate theory into noisy practice usually comes during the annual outing when teachers and

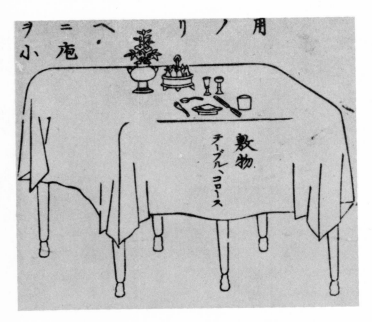

To a Japanese the dowdiness of the table cloth and the tall table legs that compete for space with his own are just as exotic as the table setting itself.

students make what is considered by all a memorable trip to one of the larger towns in their own or a neighboring prefecture. With luck the destination may be Tokyo or Osaka, and for some who live in distant rural areas it is often the only travel experience of their lives. The climax of the trip is their first brush with urbanity—a visit to a Western-style restaurant with wall-size mirrors or abstract murals and music on tap.

By then the finer points of their eating lesson have long been forgotten. No matter, youthful impetuosity wins out. All ceremonies of initiation involve the endurance of a certain amount of hardship or the contact with strange disciplines. In contrast to *mochi,* a Western meal is not pregnant with mortal danger and Japanese cutlery is notoriously blunt. More often than not, the experiment in dangerous living is a success. The young travelers in search of culture have the time of their lives and, with stomachs aching but proud of the loss of innocence, they make for home where with immense relief they return to their rice bowls and little wooden sticks.

越中滑川之大鮹

越中（ゑつちう）滑川（なめりかは）の大鮹（おほたこ）

Fishing village on the Japan Sea.

Each box contains a neatly folded human. In early times, persons of rank were carried pickaback by husky men.

Train Travel

The best time for travel in Japan were the years around the turn of the century. Barriers and chicanes of the feudal era had been abolished, and the old road system had not yet disintegrated under the abrasive wheels of buses and trucks. For a thousand years, people of every station had roved about under their own steam, shuffling along in hemp-soled sandals—armed men and merchants; peddlers, priests, and professional mendicants; pilgrims insatiate for the goodwill of enshrined deities. Overprivileged people rode in *kago,* box-like litters, which afforded them the privacy of a roomette. Moving at the pace of its bearers, *kago* was a slow and dignified way to travel. Barring a holdup, it was also the safest.

In those days roads were still veritable promenades, of easy gradient, winding up and down a succession of densely wooded hills. To be sure, some were no more than pathways offering a precarious foothold. They climbed mountain passes flanked by snow-topped peaks, forded swift rivers, cut through gorges whose perpendicular walls seemed to meet overhead. All of them held the promise of coolness. Along the seashores, even in the hot plains, a canopy of shady pines protected highways from the blazing sun. Murray's *Handbook for Travellers in Japan,* out of print for half a century but still the best source of information for the intrepid tourist, suggests dozens of journeys along the old routes, far from the railroad tracks. "The pleasantest sort of trip for a healthy man," advises the *Handbook,* "is that in which walking and jinricksha-riding are combined. In those hilly districts which make Japan so picturesque, walking is the only possible, or at least the only pleasant, method of progression."[130]

Today, wanderers have all but disappeared from high-

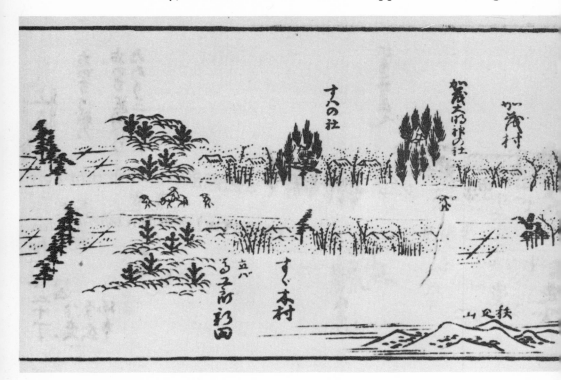

Two pages from *Kiso, the Middle Road,* 1756, a continuous, 75-foot-long map, listing the rates of lodging along the central mountain road from Kyoto to Edo (Tokyo).

ways. Pilgrims patronize country buses—rickety, springless, supremely uncomfortable contraptions—the perfect machines for doing penance. Rickshas, those gazelles among vehicles, are little more than a curiosity. In the theater districts of the big cities and occasionally near railroad stations in the northern provinces, a few battered specimens are still around, but ricksha-men are no longer willing to sign up for a week's journey.

Until rickshas made their appearance, the Japanese had never seen a wheeled vehicle. Fukuzawa, the blasé explorer of the Western world who accompanied the first Japanese ambassadors on their trip abroad, recalled among the "many confusions and embarrassing moments" of their visit to America, his first encounter with a carriage. "On

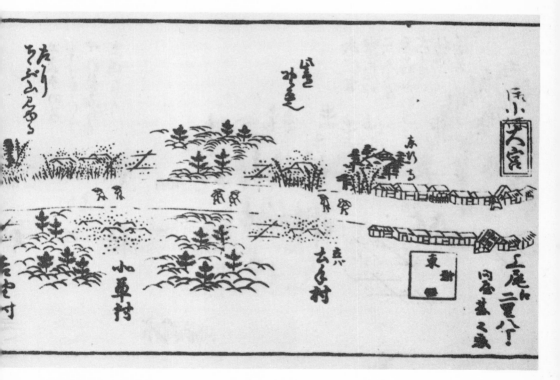

The features of the landscape—farmhouses (thatched), town houses (tiled), rice paddies, bamboo groves, and various conifers—are illustrated in a style approaching pictorial shorthand.

seeing a vehicle with horses attached to it, we should easily
have guessed what it was. But really we did not identify
our mode of conveyance until the door had been opened,
we were seated inside, and the horses had started off. Then
we realized we were riding in a carriage behind horses."[131]
When in 1870 the Japanese decided to build the first
railway, they skipped several hundred years of transportation history.

The first trains caused uproar and alarm. Not only did
the Japanese fear that railroads financed by foreign capital
would bring the country to the brink of bankruptcy, they
presented, the military were quick to point out, a convenient route for an invading enemy. (Similar fears made the
English abandon for many years all projects for a railroad
tunnel under the Channel.) Moreover, train travel gave the
Japanese their first taste of undignified transportation;
worse, it posed a threat to their mores. Temperamentally

The privacy of the traveler was assured by a hermetic, *kago*-like compartment that
had been grafted onto the Western-style carriage.

hostile to innovations that encroached on their customs, they were at a loss to know how to behave on trains. Since their vast code of etiquette provided no guidance, their traditional savoir-faire deserted them in the company of strangers in the unwished-for intimacy of a compartment. (When the first automobile—imported from France—made its début in the streets of Tokyo, its most revolutionary innovation was not the motor but the enforced presence of a travel companion of low station, the chauffeur.)

It was difficult to establish the place of trains in the order of everyday things. Although a railroad car had a roof, doors, and windows of a sort, to the Japanese way of thinking a compartment bore little resemblance to a room. It lacked the most important feature, the matted floor. To a Japanese, the floor of a house is table and chair, desk and bed. Could a train compartment be considered a room if it had no legitimate floor? Was a railroad car a house on wheels? Failure to unwind this jumble of conflicting thoughts was apt to confuse, indeed, to pervert the notions of a people thirsting for absolute certainty and famous for their politeness and fastidiousness. In the first days of rail traffic, the aforementioned Enright tells us in his *World of Dew,* "passengers behaved as they would when entering a private house. They discarded their clogs and left them in neat rows on the edge of the platform. On arriving at their destination they were shocked and aggrieved to discover that the officials had failed to pick them up and bring them along."[132]

What added to their uneasiness was the fact that the early trains lacked toilets. "Those who could not wait until they arrived at the station," writes the historian Kunio Yanagida, "were forced to relieve themselves out of the window."[133] The authorities tried to curb such inadvertency by slapping a fine on the malefactors with the result that when, in the seventh year of Japanese railroad history, toilets were installed in the trains, "most passengers thought it wrong to use them while the train was in progress." The tracks of the stations, notes Yanagida, were filthy beyond description. Although contemporary train manners lack the pungency of earlier years, they have not ceased to intrigue the Westerner. Those of us who regard travel in our own country as unrelievedly dull may find Japanese trains an unfailing source of entertainment.

Since foreign tourists patronize crack trains almost exclusively, their first impressions may be disappointing.

"Presently the train began to move forward, rolling along two lines of iron," wrote Awaji-no-Kami Muragaki of the first Japanese Embassy to the United States; "the train goes so quickly that it is almost impossible to form an idea of the country around us; it is like riding a galloping horse."

Mainliners look deceptively conventional. Chairs recline; slipcovers are stiff with starch; swivel footrests have double-faced padding—velvet for stocking- and *tabi*-feet, rubber for shod feet. At each end of the car, discreet lights indicate whether a lavatory is vacant. (There is a choice of a Western and an Oriental toilet, each decorated with flowers in a vase. One knocks on the door before entering since most Japanese are in the habit of ignoring door locks.) Throughout the car, silence prevails. From time to time it is broken by a squawk box: a female announcer, her every phrase spiked with those trills and mordents that in Japan denote the maximum of utterable politeness, recites a litany of timetables for all the trains, ferries, and buses at connecting points. The human element, however, is in limbo; congeniality is nil.

Although dining cars are common on most express trains, to eat a "foreign meal" from white plates with fork and knife is not a Japanese's idea of how to enjoy himself. The bulk of food consumed by train passengers comes in *bentô,* lunch boxes sold on the platforms of all major railroad stations. One hundred yen, the equivalent of twenty-eight American cents, buy a set of two flat wooden boxes, one filled to the brim with rice, the other containing a mosaic of tidbits for added interest rather than repletion: a piece of broiled fish, one slice of a fiercely red sausage, a tidy knot of seaweed, some pickled roots of vegetables, and maybe a snail or a shrimp. Incongruously wedged into this still life is a miniature plastic bottle with soy sauce, which the Japanese prefer to salt. With the boxes come a pair of eating sticks (still joined at one end as proof of their virginity) and a toothpick, that small but important instrument which in the hand of an expert manipulator acquires the expressiveness of a fan. *Bentô* provide, if not exactly superlative, at least stimulating food, incomparably superior to that vapid

209

foam-rubber cushion that is the American sandwich. An habitué of Japanese trains, I never met with a *bentô* that looked uninviting or did not taste good.

Stupendous quantities of these boxes are purchased by the travelers, some laying in stock that would apparently last for days. They are mostly intended for presents, although plenty of food is consumed on the spot. A *bentô* is—to borrow a word from the Japanese world of art— a *floating* collation. It has neither beginning nor end. The elegant traveler never hurries; from time to time he takes a peek at his supplies, selects a morsel from the delicacies, swallows a lump of rice, only to close the boxes and put them away. He repeats these little feedings between digestive naps for the duration of the journey. To eke out what are actually very scanty portions, he buys from ambulant girl vendors rice crackers and candy in cellophane bags and what look like Santa Claus net-stockings bulging with fruit of the season—mostly apples and tangerines.

The Japanese long ago decided that a railroad car is not a house—at least not a Japanese house—and therefore does not deserve to be treated with respect. A Western institution, it is unclean and no time is wasted driving home this point. Passengers who are not asleep are busily allaying the aseptic character of the train by fouling the floor with the refuse of their meals. Less than half an hour out of the station, the clinical atmosphere gives way to that of a Turkish marketplace. Discarded lunch boxes, wrappers, spilled rice, and fruit peelings form a soft and slippery carpet in the aisles and under the seats. This capricious form of garbage disposal is not a matter of negligence or sloth; to defile the floor of a train seems to satisfy a profound need. Gentle exhortations and educational travel posters, periodically issued by the Ministry of Transportation, have left the public unpersuaded. Hence uniformed men with armbands marked "Trainworker" (in English) are employed for the single purpose of sweeping up the garbage that collects, sometimes ankle-high, from the eating activities of the passengers. Litter does not offend a Japanese as long as it is confined to Western institutions. On the contrary, the sight of a littered waiting room in a railroad station propels him to lyric flight. To witness—a poem by Shûkei, taken from a modern anthology:

> The rubbish
> Of the waiting room
> Lifts up their legs.

Do not display educational tendencies on Japanese trains. Throw the bones on the floor—that's what the floor is for. Do not, however, throw anything out of the window— not so much as a toothpick. It may land in a rice paddy, which is sacred soil to the farmer. If Japan lured you by visions of nothing more dissolute than the litter of fallen blossoms, you will do well to ponder the power of symbols. If you set out to discover the Unspeakably Beautiful, you will have to be content with the pronouncements of flower arrangers and Zen salesmen who ply their trade as matter-of-factly as Arthur Murray's Dance Studios. The ancient Nippon of penumbras and mustiness is declining fast; the modern Japanese have set their eyes on higher aims—polluted streams, traffic jams, and blighted cities, the symbols of a civilization they are determined to make their own. The litter on trains is but a small contribution to the advancement of their underdeveloped homeland.

Crack trains and hick trains are alike in one respect: all passengers ignore each other with the finality that only Japanese are able to muster. Japanese speech, being punctilious and finely shaded from servility to haughtiness, makes it difficult to strike the appropriate conversational tone without a precise knowledge of the other's age and standing. Without these clues, social intercourse lags, neighborliness shrivels to indifference. Call it frigidity, or gaucherie, it suits everybody to perfection, all the more so as the Japanese have their own ideas on how to put travel time to the best use. By preference and inclination, they indulge in their favorite pastime: they sleep.

A short digression on sleep, native style, and the picture of the comatose Japanese is indicated at this point.

Sleep comes easy to a Japanese; he needs neither mechanical nor chemical inducement. From the moment he is born, his place is with his mother at all hours. At night he shares her bed and warmth. During her waking hours he is strapped to her back, providing her with perfect balance in the sense of both equipoise and counterweight. Sometimes the baby's head swings like a pendulum from her back, as if his neck were broken, yet it is all in the line of learning early in life how to steal a nap. There are no cradles in Japan.

The growing child is taught to acquire a statue's poise. At night, his head is confined to a rigid support. Instead of snuggling up to a downy cushion, he must place his neck on a hard square pillow, a bag filled with unhusked grain. There are many refinements of this torture. Formerly, pillows were made of wood. In the old days, when families were blessed with many more children than today, "the young people or apprentices slept with their heads on a log and the father or employer would strike one end of it with a hammer to wake them up."[134] Never to let his head slide off the pillow is among the cardinal rules of a child's training. Since he has no bed or bunk to himself but shares the floor with his family, he learns not to trespass upon their claims and attains a virtuosity in sleeping that makes other nationals insomniacs by comparison. Throughout his life, his capacity for sleep remains undiminished. "Sleeping," wrote Ruth Benedict, "is one of the most accomplished arts of the Japanese. They sleep with complete relaxation, in any position, under any circumstances we regard as sheer impossibility."[135]

Day trains are traveling exhibitions of this incomparable skill. Benches barely seating two—too short for even the shortest man to stretch out—seem to provide exactly the right touch of discomfort that makes a nap only that much more desirable: the wooden armrest is just hard and high enough to serve as pillow, and passengers walking through the aisle forever brush against the cantilevered heads. This works as a challenge to bring out the consummate talents of a champion sleeper.

Although indifferent to what we call sleeping comfort, a Japanese does not like to keep his clothes on when traveling in the warm season. It is not uncommon for a man to undress right after boarding a train, to unbutton his

Kago means, literally, basket, and its occupant must indeed have looked like a basket case. Today's traveler has preserved his ancestors' adaptability.

trousers, step out of them, and put them, together with his jacket, neatly folded into the baggage rack; to take off his shirt, slip out of shoes and socks, and, averse as he is to sitting on chairs and benches with his legs dangling, to pull up his feet onto his seat or, better yet, stick them out of the window. By dint of some organ, unknown to and unsuspected by non-Japanese, he is able, even when profoundly asleep, to intercept warning signals and thus, without awakening, to retract his feet for the few moments of the passing of another train.

Occasionally though, this guileless world of sleep becomes the bane of the foreign traveler. Among the truly irksome habits of a Japanese is his insistence on sleeping in total darkness. At nightfall, the heavy wooden shutters of his house are hermetically closed and not until he rises are they opened again. Unlike the frail slatted porte-fenêtres of Mediterranean countries which distill the light into a sort of optical liqueur, Japanese outer doors are made in the manner of bulwarks, to ward off sound, light, and burglars. What a Japanese dreads most is the night air, believed to be lethal to a sleeping person. The Western tourist who puts up at a Japanese house is in for a fit of claustrophobia.

Nothing, however, equals his consternation on entering a day train to find it blacked out for the benefit of somnolent passengers. Any attempt at having a peak at the outdoors by raising a shade as little as an inch is thwarted by his fellow passengers who will angrily jerk it shut. Although the Japanese are perhaps the world's sight-seeingest people, they have peculiar notions on what merits their attention. They have rigidly graded their country's scenery and, year after year, generation after generation, return with undiminished enthusiasm to the officially accredited sights. But *while* they are traveling, they will not waste their time with gazing at a non-pedigreed landscape.

Nevertheless, train travel has its compensations. If the landscape is often illusive, the human element is not. Despite the splendid isolation of the passengers, the cobweb of human relationships is palpably real. Travel is a good occasion for testing one's social status and popularity.

The departure by train of an important man is steeped in ceremony. For him, travel is not a private affair but a public event. On the station platform, facing the honorable window, farewell platoons composed of relatives, friends, colleagues and subalterns, are standing motionless, suspended in space and time—a monument in the flesh. The atmosphere is one of unrelieved solemnity. No valedictorian speeches mar the silent communication of spirits. Pent-up emotions remain pent-up. Even the end of the vigil brings no release. A bedlam of bells and whistles heralding zero hour merely draws the subject of all the attention to the window. Nobody cheers; the sight of the august passenger sends flurries of violent bowing through the ranks, like gusts of wind whipping a wheatfield. Only when the window recedes in the distance do the well-wishers regain their upright position.

The ceremony is repeated at every train stop. The dozing big shot is discreetly awakened by his henchmen to receive the homage of another batch of local supernumeraries. Again, no speeches are made, no vulgar display of affections shown. The purity of the relationship is expressed, as it were, in statistics.

At the height of winter, this ritual takes on a masochistic note since Japanese etiquette demands that an obeisance never be made with one's outer garments on. Even a scarf around one's neck impairs a salutation's authenticity. A delegation standing at attention on a railway platform is a sight to remember: overcoats over their arms, puffing clouds of breath into the icy air, while the subject in whose honor so much mortification is perpetrated sits, drowsy from the heat, behind a hermetically closed window opaque from condensation. The foreigner, tempted to commiserate with the victims of Japanese etiquette, is relieved to learn that three sets of underwear do not show more than one.

These manifestations of loyalty and pomp seem puny, however, compared to those that brightened travel in

Part of a daimyô's procession.

former times. "The train with which the princes of the Empire visit Edo (present-day Tokyo)," wrote Siebold, "amount in number to 10,000 men for those of the lowest rank, and 20,000 for those of the highest."[136] The *Tokaido* Highway, the *camino real* of feudal Japan, which linked Kyoto with Yedo, was as busy as a modern metropolitan thoroughfare during the rush hour. In fact, the Japanese were the first to establish modern traffic regulations. "Their

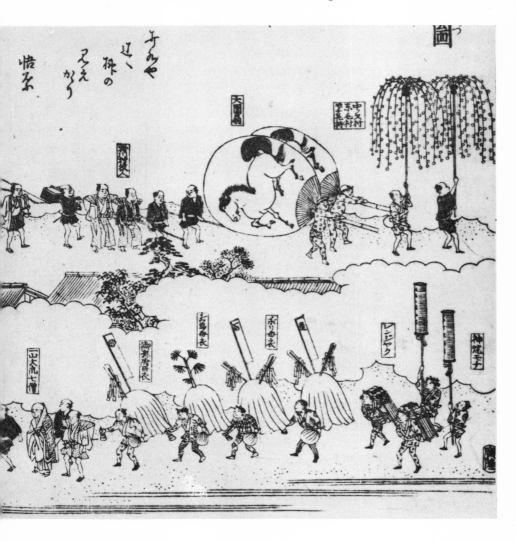

care for good order and the convenience of travelers," wrote the physician Thunberg who visited Japan in the 1770s, "has gone so far that those who travel up the country always keep to the left, and those that come from the capital, to the right; a regulation which would be of the greatest utility in Europe."[137] Since everybody progressed at the same pace—even today, to overtake a person walking in the street is considered ill-mannered—it was easy to observe the right of way. What threw the excellent arrangement out of kilter was the prevailing travel etiquette.

Precedence posed problems within the same caravan, making it practically impossible for two important people to proceed side by side. (Not even in our day do a well-bred Japanese husband and wife walk abreast. Japan's crown prince, the living symbol of emancipation, walks five paces ahead of his consort.) Thus, although a high dignitary traveled with many attendants, his constant companion was loneliness.

Problems of who takes precedence over whom were magnified when two caravans met head-on. Observance of respect for rank was rigidly enforced; the rabble had to prostrate themselves and not raise their eyes until the gentry was out of sight. For a man jealously guarding his position, such encounters were fraught with peril since arguments used to be settled by swords rather than words. This enlivened travel and kept the men in fine shape.

Not surprisingly, foreigners experienced difficulties in clearing these ceremonial roadblocks. A foreign traveler encountering a native lord was to dismount his horse and show his skill in kowtowing, a requirement which sometimes led to fatal accidents. Only ten years before the opening of the Yokohama-Tokyo railway, right on the highway that runs parallel to its tracks, an Englishman in the company of a lady and two compatriots, got in the way of the procession of a feudal lord and, his conduct being found unsatisfactory, was put to death by the offended party. Such clashes of Eastern and Western travel etiquette would have seemed unavoidable were it not that by then the ancient code of chivalry was on its way out. Trains spelled the end of the old morality.

Train travel made the enforcement of the good old manners impossible. For one thing, it was absurd to divide the nation into three classes. For another, how could people encountering each other at the combined speed of two trains moving in opposite directions pay their respects to an important person! A last vestige of the native *pudor* can perhaps be discerned in the fact that to this day the majority of Japanese railway lines run on a single track.

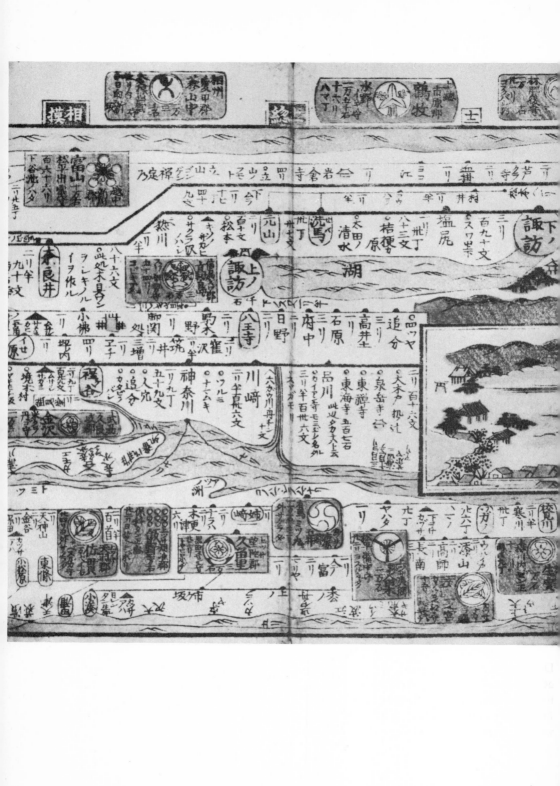

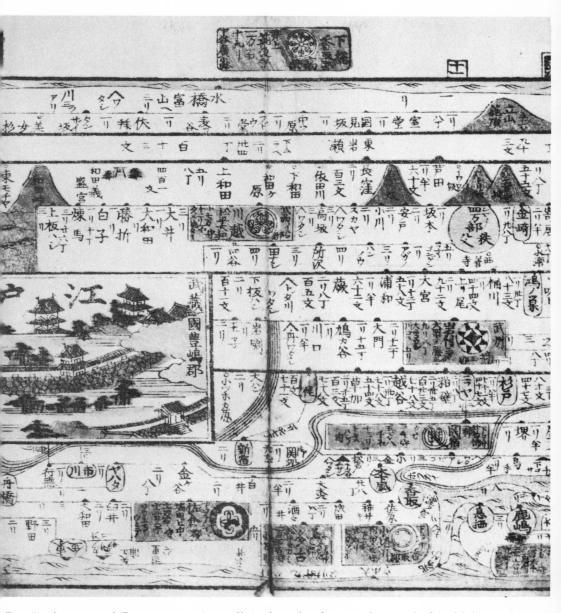

Detail of a map of Japan, 1722. Accordion-pleated color woodcut, 7 inches high, 26 feet long. To fit the odd format, the shape of the country had to be elongated to about ten times its length. The Pacific Ocean (bottom) and the Japan Sea (top) are reduced to border lines. Roads run parallel, mountains mimic Fuji. The various territories are identified by the crests of clans.

Taste by Edict

To have or not to have taste is a question raised compellingly, almost hypnotically, by Japan, where taste is one of the oldest national institutions. Born into a country abounding in those elements of nature that stimulate the practice of poetry and the formation of a sensitive soul—mountains, seas and four unmistakable seasons—the Japanese have perfected methods of distilling beauty from these riches to a degree unknown to us. What is more, they have succeeded in codifying beauty. Among Japanese there is no disputing of tastes.

But first we have to persuade ourselves—in defiance of the puritanical and cynical authorities of the world of art —that the subject of taste must not be lightly dismissed. Does taste really matter?

Emphatically yes. Call a man a murderer or a thief without being able to show cause and you will incur imprisonment or mulct, or both, as a matter of course; the point—implied but never exactly stated—being that the penalty helps the offender to redeem his guilt. Accuse a man, justly or not, of having bad taste and you commit an inexpiable crime. Unless the victim dies a sudden death, say, of apoplexy, he faces a life made miserable by slow poisoning; the verbal infamy lingers on while the offender goes free. The reason why no action can be brought against the imputation of bad taste lies in our permanent confusion in all matters of taste. Although taste is sold over the counter in a number of adulterations, so far it is not available in its pure form. Like certain viruses, it has never been isolated from its carrier. It cannot be laid on or peeled off. It suffuses, as it were, an object or a person like a halo, albeit perceptible to the true believer only.

To judge from historical evidence, questions of taste have occupied the minds of men more intensely than questions of immortality or of the purpose of life. Yet the precise nature of taste eludes philosopher and philistine alike. No definition of good taste has ever met with universal acceptance. Wise men, trying to discover its laws, threw up their hands after a lifetime of disputes and declared that there is no accounting for taste. Their verdict was caused by ignorance; they had never heard of Japan where good taste was endemic almost within living memory.

To understand a country as distant and outlandish as Japan, every generation has to rediscover it, for all knowledge is imperfect and impermanent, oozing away through the sands of time when not ceaselessly refreshed and replenished. Hence, today as in the past, seekers of beauty are converging on Japan to re-examine its assets in the light of the aesthetic revolution that has taken place in the Western world during the past thirty years.

Their chances are poor. Their thirst for knowledge remains unassuaged for it is difficult to recognize Japanese taste in its bewildering diversity, and, more important, to grasp the *ethical* substance in Japanese aesthetics. In Japan, taste was never considered a luxury; it is perfectly compatible with poverty. After all, it was the poor man's taste that prevailed over the rich. Unfortunately we know little about the poor peoples' lives in former times. The vision is clouded by the selectiveness of the chroniclers. Like their modern colleagues, they seldom bothered with the little man. They put their best efforts into recording the easy circumstances of the well-to-do.

It is therefore difficult to conjure up from the mists of history a picture of the Japanese who lived ten centuries before our time, all the more so because they correspond to our idea of the Japanese as little as the Chinese or the Indians do. What shall we make of Japanese gentlemen who wound strings of beads around their necks and legs, and put flowers in their hair like bacchic Greeks— surely, a shocking thing to do in the eyes of the mournful present-day Japanese. Or of women wearing their hair long, loose and trailing on the floor, looking for all one knows like retired maenads, rendered corpulent and blowsy by a sedentary life. Their costumes were beguilingly rich and exotic—women in artichoke-like court dresses so ample that one of them filled a small apartment; men in what one might call self-transcendent pantaloons twice as long as their legs, the surplus being dragged on the ground as in a sack race. Still, these clothes and ornaments no more expressed individual taste than do the uniform and medals of a modern soldier. Sartorial do's and don'ts were dictated by the government.

To judge from the regulations for the ranks of bureaucracy, no less than two hundred and sixteen varieties of dress were in use. The task of designing them was not left to the whims of tailors and hatters but was assigned to the lawmakers themselves. A bureau of etiquette prescribed the correct outfits of eighteen different categories of princes, thirty ranks of officers, and so forth, all the way down to the lowliest supernumerary. The shape, color and texture

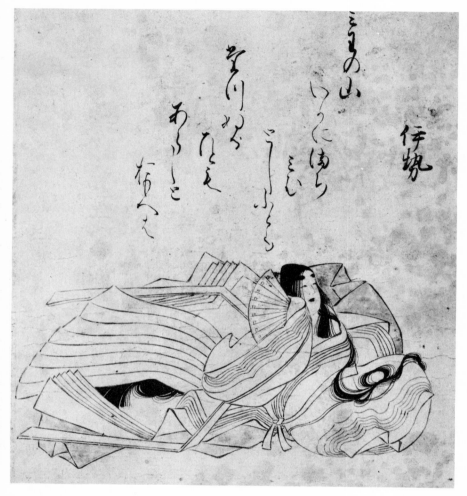

Whatever the opposite of a form-fitting dress, this is it—*juni-hitoe*, the many-layered costume of a court lady. The face, the only visible part of the body, was painted chalk-white, the teeth blackened. Eyebrows were shaved (as were nose and cheeks) and appeared several inches higher in bold facsimile. The long, jet-black tresses disappeared and re-emerged like Istrian rivers. From a scroll of the Kamakura Period (twelfth to fourteenth century).

Courtesy, Spencer Collection, The New York Public Library.

of the garments, the size of the stitches and number of knots were defined by edicts whose nonobservance entailed severe punishment. Women as well as men were denied the pleasure and privilege of selecting their own clothes. Withal, the codification of taste seemed to have no adverse effect on the upper classes who carried on in tasteful abandon.

Their houses were perhaps a trifle on the Spartan side. Domestic architecture was lowly, not to say elementary, little resembling the one we are familiar with. All the elements that we consider characteristically Japanese—sliding doors, paper screens, rice-straw mats—were still of the future. Even the aristocracy of the prosperous Heian Period (ninth to twelfth centuries) occupied dwellings not much

Short legs look even shorter in overlong trousers, yet true costume emphasizes rather than hides body chracteristics. The trailing pantaloons were intended to curtail the wearer's mobility, a wise precaution in an age of excessive sword play. A drawing by Ichirûsai Hiroshige (1797–1858).

different from farmhouses. But then, since conspicuous display was despised by all, not much distinction was intended.

Hardly any architecture of the early times has survived; Japanese buildings do not produce ruins for a number of reasons. For one thing, buildings disappear periodically in conflagrations caused by earthquakes or negligence (only to rise phoenix-like, if ever so anachronistically, from the ashes). For another, setting a building on fire is a common form of protest with the Japanese, like picketing with us. Their propensity for destruction is sometimes worked off in rituals: unwilling to wait for lightning to strike or some such sign from the gods, they tear down the Great Ise Shrines every twenty years to rebuild them in their identical image. Apart from a strong vein of arson, there is an entire web of pathological streaks in the Japanese—delayed-action revenge, self-immolation, suicide out of spite, ceremonial lunacy, and all the elementary destructiveness of the problem child. All these dusky complexes came to the fore with apocalyptical force at that fatal moment in history when, giving way to the pressure of foreign powers, the Japanese decided on their own peculiar version of Westernization. Sensing in their artistic heritage obstacles to their emancipation from the past, they simply decided to do away with them. Thus, the era called, ironically, the Restoration, saw the most organized and most successful demolition of national monuments, not exceeded even in the last war.

First to go were the castles; of the several hundred no more than a few survived the purge. Of course, castles had long lost their military importance but they often constituted the only ennobling feature in an otherwise monotonous townscape; although patterned after European fortifications, they had none of their grimness. Not to be outdone by the soldiery, civic authorities did their patriotic share by sacking imperial palaces, if only because "to deface antique works of art was considered a sign of civilization and progress."[138] The third among the raiding forces, Shinto priests, converged on ecclesiastical buildings. They summarily despoiled or razed Buddhist temples and their treasure houses, and replaced them with buildings dedicated to the state religion. In short, the first years of Westernization were a period of self-inflicted calamities. Lacking a precedent for correct procedure, the Japanese prepared for the new era by committing cultural suicide.

To ask why nobody spoke up against the desecration of the old is to ignore the workings of the Japanese mind. Protesting is considered an abominable action, regardless of the motive. "Strength of character," Ruth Benedict pointed out, "is shown in conforming, not in rebelling; nonconformity brings humiliation and ridicule." This reversal of the concepts of courage and cowardice often defeats our attempts to understand educated Japanese.

Another question altogether is what happened to Japanese national pride at the time of the cultural blackout. Since artistic monuments have a symbolic value besides their monetary worth, the willful destruction casts doubt on their power of discrimination, let alone their sanity. Only when we reflect on the difference between their and our relationship to works of art, does their behavior appear somewhat less puzzling.

Occidentals have, or pretend to have, a ravenous appetite for art in all its manifestations. An eyeful of beauty is not enough; what counts is quantity. Even people who are usually unsusceptible to the charms of art are known to trudge through the world's great museums in the hope of aesthetic indulgence. Square miles of canvas are grazed with glassy eyes, canyons of marble and bronze traversed between breakfast and lunchtime, to no avail and no effect other than tired feet and visual constipation.

This peripatetic style of communing with art, if no longer unknown to the Japanese in this age of industrial tourism, is temperamentally uncongenial to them. They do not like to take art on the run; they sit down to it, much as they do to a meal. Above all, they like to treat it as a private affair. A collector of traditional art who lives in a traditional house does not scatter his treasures all over the place but keeps them, literally, under wraps. To look at a hanging scroll he first has to extract it from a box. (Precious objects are often encased in veritable nesting sets of boxes.) He then frees it of its silken wrappings with gestures as measured as in the tea ceremony, and displays it in an appropriate alcove, the *tokonoma*. Once up on the wall, the scroll is approached on one's knees and gazed at, dreamily rather than critically, with the sort of awe usually extended to holy pictures. This reverie, together with the time-consuming task of unwrapping and rewrapping, is a trial of patience for a non-Japanese. To see all the treasures of a well-endowed monastery— provided permission for such undertaking were given at all —might require the better part of a year.

Not only were art collections out of reach for the poor man, Japan never had the equivalent of our art for the masses, such as ecclesiastical art—no Giottos, no Bosches, no luminous stained-glass windows with the power to transport the mind of the beholder into another world. Japanese temples are mostly devoid of pictorial art. The famous mausolea of Nikko are perhaps closest to our own liberal architecture: accessible, rather garish in an enjoyable way. They are comparable to that Athenian Acropolis we do not quite dare to visualize—not today's bleached ruins but the pristine buildings, gaudily painted and all

229

but hidden by a holy grove. Moreover, Japan never had any civic architecture to speak of—no fora, no cool arcades or gorgeous fountains—for the simple reason that they never had any use for it. Their tastes were essentially rustic. Connoisseurship was conditioned (and often limited) to their natural environment. All these circumstances may help to explain their apathy toward the destruction of their national monuments.

Like languages, taste is best acquired in childhood. In Japan, a child's aesthetic sensibilities are awakened long before he is introduced to social duties. The education available to him still perpetuates that of older generations who subscribed to the Socratic principle (formulated independently) that "the aim and consummation of all education is the love of loveliness." In Japan, nature has not altogether lost its paradisiac loveliness—a tree is not primarily lumber, a river not essentially a sewer. Although a Japanese never yields to the kind of paroxysm of admiration some Westerners suffer when communing with nature, he seldom will abuse it.

Nature is a Japanese child's playground and toy shop.

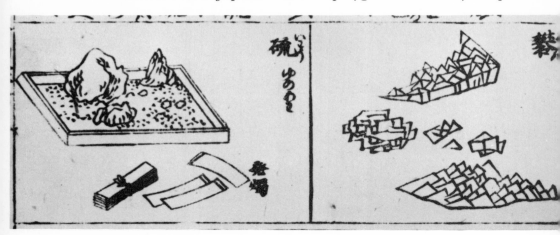

Minerals from a seventeenth-century encyclopedia: sulfur, magnet (*sic*), alum-shale, sardonyx, and brimstone.

Yet he is told to keep at a proper distance. He is not allowed to go barefoot outdoors or sit on the ground. He must wear a hat in summer, carry an umbrella in the rain. Thus, his mind is early impregnated with ideas of cleanliness bordering on primness that in time become to him as natural as they remain strange to us: he does not distinguish between what is aesthetically beautiful and hygienically clean. In his language, clean stands for beautiful, and vice versa.

His is not merely a case of clean fingernails and a washed neck. Cleanliness has other implications. Unlike a Western child, he stays away from animals. The station that we accord a dog has no analogy in Japanese life. The thought of tolerating a dog on one's premises, making it the playmate of children, can only spring, a Japanese thinks, from a depraved mind. To him, a dog is a lascivious animal. Even on a farm, animals and humans are unconditionally segregated, and although a peasant may be sentimentally attached to his ox, he does not invite it to his house.

This devotion to cleanliness represents no doubt the most

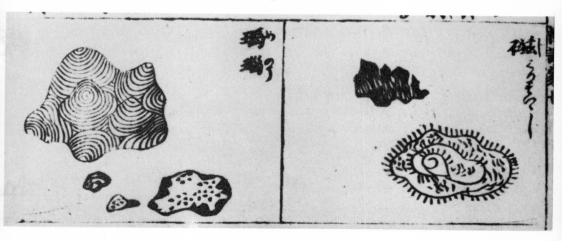

appealing of all their tastes. It is also the least exportable one. At the age of eighteen months, when the child learns to use eating sticks, he is taught an elementary religious-aesthetic commandment—to eat everything that is served; to treat food with a respect that among us is reserved for the consecrated wafer only. To him, food is a divine gift, not just edible matter. If he grows up in the farm country where there still is a great deal of propitiating of good and evil spirits, he prays to the rice god. Later in life, he may undertake a pilgrimage to pay his respects to the Goddess of Food. So deeply does regard for food and fastidiousness in handling it become ingrained in him that he is incapable of making a mess of it. That is, when it comes to eating a Japanese meal served in Japanese style. When he sits down to a Western-style meal, his rules find no application because to him such a meal is *a priori* unaesthetic. Whenever the need arises, he takes to Western customs—even what he regards as repulsive ones—to the point of cheerfulness. But at bottom he despises them. His equation of Westerners with "dirt" and "pollution" is not a squeamish metaphor but the aesthetic-hygienic rating that he assigns us in his scale.

In the eyes of a Japanese there is no excuse for our habit of leaving part of the food uneaten *on the plate,* thereby converting it into garbage right on the dining table. To him, this is as blasphemous as it is unappetizing. In fact, he is surprised that it causes us no qualms. No flicker of embarrassment crosses our faces when we commit the ultimate outrage of homespun etiquette by *stacking* dirty dishes.

National pride manifests itself to no small degree in upholding, if need be defending, one's customs regardless of their merits. Among us, the integrity of the citizen is often judged by the intensity of his contempt for alien customs and his uncritical acceptance of national ones. When he lives or travels abroad, the maxims inherited from his ancestors provide him with a formidable armor that in times of crisis is polished to blinding perfection. Yet although it shields the obtuse, it is of no use to the open-minded. "There comes a point," writes Miss Vining—who has a firsthand knowledge of the perils of Japan—"when anyone who has spent considerable time in the Orient must decide which he is going to do: yield to its charms and become faintly but indelibly imbued with its point of view and subtly yet unmistakably cut off from the currents of thought and feeling in occidental countries, or break away and go home before it is too late."[139] Too late for what?

Alas, instead of shedding our ideological reservations, if only for the brief time of a visit to Japan, and making the best of both worlds, we merely try to cover them up with a whiff of connoisseurship—a sort of cultural deodorant—and, finding Oriental aesthetics confusing, turn to that great open-air market of taste, Japanese nature.

Again, this proves unrewarding for we are not on easy terms with nature. Preoccupied mainly with the antagonistic forces between man and nature, we fail to perceive the eternal harmonies and rhythms. Much as we set store on book knowledge, we neglect to educate our senses. Charles Darwin, a matchless observer of nature, remarked that no animal is capable of admiring a beautiful landscape or the heavens at night. Neither, he said, are barbarians and uneducated persons; "such tastes are acquired through culture and depend on complex associations."[140]

Complex associations are the chief characteristic of the Japanese worship of nature. There is no malice in saying that the Japanese love nature best when it follows art. Uncouth, uncontrolled nature evokes little response in them. Gardens rather than groves tally with their ideal blueprint for good taste. A pinch of abstraction, a few touches of symbolism, greatly help to attune nature to their aesthetic wavelength. Some of their horticultural philosophy can be inferred from temple- and palace-gardens—those empty lots, bepebbled and berocked according to esoteric rules, where fortunes are spent on stones not much bigger than a potato and hardly different in shape. Maybe we ought to envy the imaginative powers of a people who can distinguish rocks by one hundred and thirty-eight names (if only two sexes); that will court and covet rocks of special appeal, kidnap them, wrap them in silks and brocades like the most precious of sweethearts, and carry them in triumphal procession to their new abode. This makes for an exciting lore but somehow the lofty examples of their art of gardening smack of the taxidermist rather than the gardener.

My own sympathies lean toward the plebeian gardens that Japanese city dwellers cultivate in their backyards. Kept up with an outlay of pennies, they nevertheless permit their owners to bring into play all the consummate *tact* that guides their relationship to growing things and, next to cleanliness, is the chief ingredient of their traditional taste. What could be more aesthetic (in the sense of the appreciation of the beautiful) than their precautions of clothing trees and bushes with coats of straw against the winter cold; of providing them with artful umbrellas to lessen the weight of snow on their branches; of nursing typhoon-damaged trees back to health by bandaging their wounds and fitting them with crutches? Such charitableness is not shared by the most soft-hearted of our garden club members. *Our* arboreal cripples are unceremoniously retired to the garbage heap. In our country the spell of nature blows away with the first autumn storms. Green thumbs turn blue, the Garden Beautiful becomes a graveyard and we draw the curtains.

A group of desirable, meaningful rocks from a book on gardening.

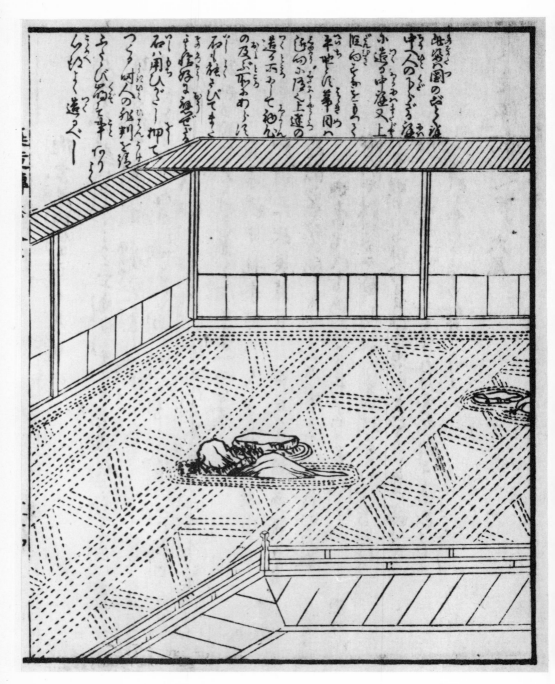

The notorious sand garden of Ryôanji Temple near Kyoto. The dotted lines of the woodcut convey the eerie beauty of the sand patterns far better than do photographs. From an undated garden book.

真之石組之庭之圖

Unlike us, a Japanese knows how to enjoy his garden all the year round. The wintery picture of a traditional house, its walls wide open, the inmates hypnotized by the spectacle of falling snow, is far less eccentric than it would seem at first. People whose recipes for pleasure include snow-viewing are likely to live in old-fashioned, unheated houses whose indoor temperature does not much differ from that outdoors. However, the fences surrounding the garden shut out cold winds and let the slow-falling flakes settle on the buttressed and corseted trees, completing their mummery.

Another form of Japanese aesthetic fancy—more osten-

The most cherished flowers are the blossoms of the fifty varieties of the Japanese cherry tree, *prunus serrulata.*

tatious, if slightly deprecated—is cherry blossom viewing. Over the years it has developed from a simple act of nature worship into Japan's most popular spectator sport. Much misunderstood by foreigners, it nevertheless figures high on the list of tourist lures. "A traveler visiting Japan in March," suggests the *Official Guide,* "should, if he begins his itinerary at Nagasaki or Shimonoseki [both in the South], so time his tour as to be able to see the cherry-blossoms at their best all through the country, from Kyoto to Nara, to Yoshino, and finally to Tokyo and its vicinity."[141] Newspapers carry daily reports on the cherry trees since it is all-important to catch the very instant of maximum efflo-

rescence. Each year the Japanese travel en masse to these accredited places, and when the infatuation reaches a pitch, induced and sustained as much by the wondrous sight of multipetaled blossoms as by the consumption of magnums of rice-wine, they seem to be mystically joined to nature. Some of them gather and preserve the blossoms for making tea that is all but tasteless. It is an elegant conceit like *mushi-zuke,* rice-wine in which vipers have

Alfresco parties at cherry-blossom time.

been kept for some time to add a flavor of daring. Underprivileged people who cannot afford to see the authentic trees in bloom reserve their gurgles of pleasure for the plastic cherry blossoms that, wired to dead branches, are put up in the city streets.

The ritualistic contemplation of flowering trees, of a snowfall or a full moon, betray some essential qualities of Japanese taste. On the whole, this taste is frugal rather than expensive, collective rather than individual. Above all, it is highly selective. There are flowers to be admired and flowers to be ignored, mountains to be climbed and mountains to be spurned, but in no instance is the choice left to the individual. Nothing pains a Japanese more than the indiscriminate admiration that foreigners lavish on his country.

On the other hand, nature's magic eludes us even in its most obvious manifestations. We would think, for instance, that the moon looks pretty much the same to the citizens of Kyoto or Kansas City; and that they take much the same pleasure in her soft light. Such, however, is not the case. Surely tastes are bound to be uneven, yet what shall we make of the fact that our poets render homage to the moon in *all* her shapes, and lovers get moonstruck *all* the year round, whereas in Japan only a full moon merits attention, and not just any full moon either. Just as a French housewife shopping for a ripe Camembert will pass up a dozen boxes in her search for the one perfect piece, the Japanese skip eleven months until comes the mid-August Moon (of the old lunar calendar) that alone suits their taste to perfection. It is—to believe them—the one and only full moon that is just a little bigger, a trifle rounder, a bit more mature, in short, *à point*. In that magical night, people forgo part of their sleep, brave the dreaded night air, and join in contemplating the celestial body.

Japanese taste being in the public domain—it never bears a personal stamp—clichés of beauty are not only of the essence but assume the status of a law. To say that a Japanese prefers a chrysanthemum to a rose is to miss the point. For him to breed roses is probably as unseemly as for an American to develop a knowledge of wines. Chrysanthemums have been bred for fifteen centuries whereas roses, being of foreign extraction, never made the grade.

Given the inexpensiveness of nature's spectacle, some foreigners have been tempted to trace Japanese taste to an ingrained sense of frugality. Others, going one step further, advanced the thought that Japanese taste is the natural consequence of an age-old poverty. Indeed, so convincing does this explanation seem that the Japanese have not hesitated to make it their own. At least, they do little to discredit it. "It was because they were so poor that the Japanese discovered a world of beauty unknown to Western aesthetics," says a student in a novel by Osaragi; "they had been denied the luxury of really satisfying their human desires, so they suppressed them and found ways to enjoy poverty."[142]

This is a hazardous assumption. If poverty begets aesthetic supermen, the nineteenth-century Irish might easily have outranked their Japanese contemporaries. The mistake lies in equating poverty as force majeure with poverty as self-discipline. The first is exemplified by a people in the throes of famine, the other by a rich man entering the mendicant orders. Yet self-abnegation is so rare as to be written off as a mental disorder. Healthy men—the Japanese included—have a healthy appetite for life's riches, and no solemn commandments, no folksy wisdom or noble precepts will make them embrace a beggarly, albeit aesthetic, existence. For that they need stronger medicine. The miracle that brought about Japanese taste—at any rate,

Chrysanthemum exhibitions are held during the first three weeks in November. A single plant may blossom with a thousand flowers, or produce half a dozen colors and varieties on one stem.

the sort of taste we have reason to envy them—was *legislated austerity,* and, since this is never mentioned (the Japanese are silent on this point), my own theory is presented herewith for what it is worth.

Sumptuary laws regulating the standard and style of living, often down to small details, were part and parcel of almost every old civilization. Sparta, famous for the scantiness of dress and brevity of speech of its people, became a byword for severity. So did Puritan. In a world devoid of the blessings of advertising, the early English settlers had no difficulty in imposing parsimony on each other by coercion. The Japanese distinguish themselves merely for having enacted sumptuary laws of a variety and minuteness unparalleled in history.

The early edicts were, as we have seen, sumptuary laws in reverse. Instead of restraining luxury, they encouraged it. The laws that shaped—one might say, copyrighted—Japanese taste were concerned with regulating the expenditures of the humble. (The merchant class was able to live in what came nearest to luxury.) From the seventeenth century on, Japanese peasants, who made up the bulk of the population, enjoyed a certain prosperity. With no wars to fight, the military rulers consolidated their power by creating a foolproof system of agriculture. The use of the soil, storage of food and standards of living were subject to strictly enforced regulations. Since the Japanese farmer was essentially a human machine for growing rice, his status was defined by his production potential. A harvest of five hundred bushels entitled him to live in a house sixty feet long, provided it had no parlor and the roof was not tiled. But he was not permitted to eat rice. Although he may have been breeding silkworms, he had to wear cotton clothes. The quality of the straw that went into the making of his raincoat was as accurately prescribed

Rice harvest.

六郷家

藤原政乗 下ニアリ 六郷兵庫ス
政勝 ニサイクラ 伊賀守
友迪 トモニミチ 藤若衛門
某 外記

御宿場
上野福聚院 増上寺 月窓院
下赤坂田町西角

二万千百石余居城肥後球麻郡舎

本名球戸郡人吉城ト云江戸ゟ大坂マテ陸百州ゟ余六坂ゟ筑前
かまつらゟ糸ニテ海上百六三ゟ鯰河原ゟ肥後国佐鋪マテ陸四七
里佐鋪ゟ人吉ニテ山路八里都合三百廿ゟ余

當城差出之高慶長十ゟ相良氏代々領之

六郷兵庫頭政経 朝散太夫

上浅草観音後 大手ヰ平町
御内室阿部伊豫守正右妹
献上蝋燭一箱銀四枚奉府
拝領巻物五 末御暇

月人 太田与左ェ門 村 山内吟右ェ門 萩賀堂右ェ門

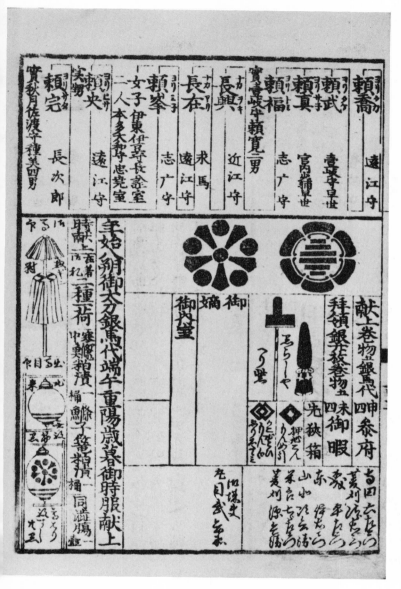

The style of living of the upper classes was firmly established. Their insignias, crests, the markings of all ceremonial paraphernalia—banners, lanterns, costumes—were listed and illustrated in social registers, complete with genealogical information.

Two pages from a directory of feudal lords. Early 1830s.

as was the wood for building his house or the clay for his cups. The sort of lanterns and flowerpots he owned, the wooden hairpins worn by his wife, his children's toys, were decreed by the government. Neither food, clothes nor shelter was left to his choice. The laws were still in force one hundred years ago when they astonished Townsend Harris by their intricacy. "It would be an endless task," he declared, "to attempt to put down all the acts of a Japanese that are regulated by authority."[143]

Harris, the envoy of a country eager to share the happiness of its citizens with the rest of the world, found the Japanese a poor target for charity. "They are all fat, well clad and happy looking," he noted in his diary, "but there is an equal absence of any appearance of wealth or of poverty,—a state of things that may perhaps constitute the real happiness of a people. I sometimes doubt whether the opening of Japan to foreign influences will promote the *general happiness* of this people. It is more like the golden age of simplicity and honesty than I have seen in any other country."[144] Harris is an eloquent example of the low-resistance American that Miss Vining would have been anxious to see repatriated. He liked what he saw and made no bones about it; in the Japanese perspective, sumptuary laws compared favorably with free enterprise. "This," Harris wrote, anticipating Veblen's scorn for conspicuous display, "is no country for modistes, tailors, jewelers and the whole army that batten on the *imaginary* wants of the West."[145] (Our italics.)

Japan's rulers did not stop at providing for the physical wants of the people but also furnished guidance in matters of conduct. Not even a holiday mood was exempt from legislation; the shogun Yoshimune laid down the rule that "getting up great excitement at a festival is forbidden." Gaiety was never in good taste among the Japanese, and

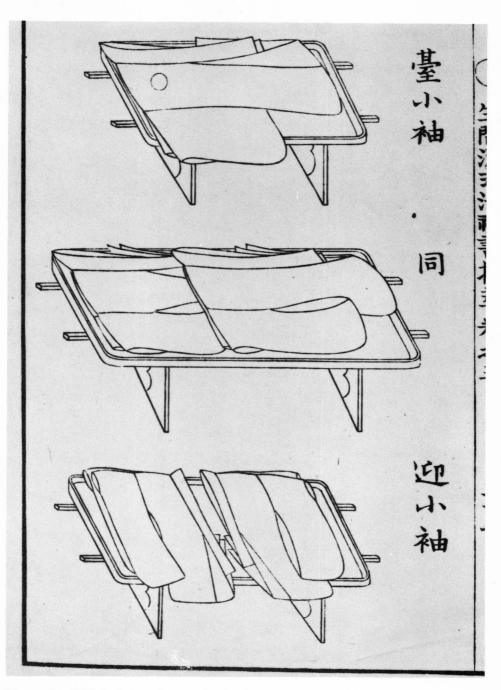

臺小袖・同

迎小袖

Trays with folded clothes. From a book of etiquette for women, 1660.

里乃子の
君ミやう
いさむ
鼓うち

其角

Street procession from an early nineteenth century book.

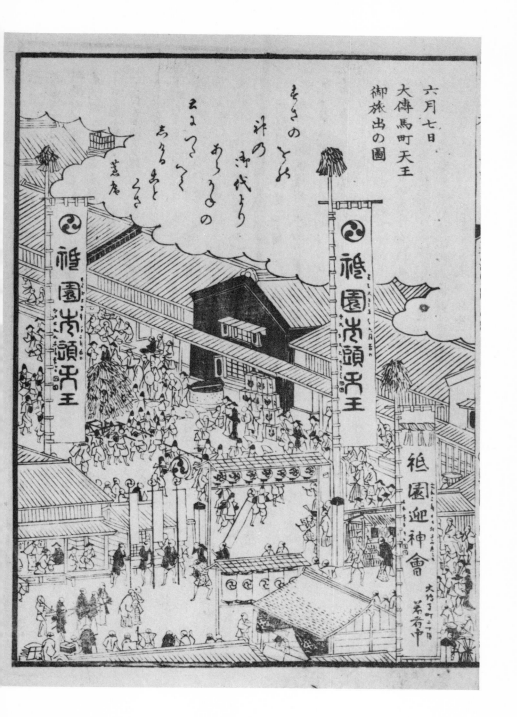

六月七日
大傳馬町天王
御旅出の圖

もゝきの
祥の
御代より
あらゝの
云ふくくの
ありくくあと
くき

荒店

祇園牛頭天王

祇園牛頭天王

祇園迎神會

大傳馬町二丁目
若者中

even today, free as they are on the whole to do what they like, one can detect an asthmatic note in their merriment.

For the little man the benefits of legislated taste far outweighed the restrictions. Not only did the law endow him with an excruciating sensibility, it stifled greed, and relieved him of worries that poisoned less fortunate peoples' lives. A farmer was able to marry off his daughter with a dowry that amounted to little more than a first aid kit (two chests, enough wicker to make a basket, a wine jug, a sash and a fan) and get away with a wedding dinner consisting mostly of soup, without being called a niggard. He never knew the anguish of choosing the appropriate gift when visiting a relative; he did not have to squabble with his servants about the amount of their wages since wages and gifts were established by the letter of the law. Above all, there was no need to keep up with the Joneses when no one was allowed to enlarge his house or acquire new land. Indeed, it cost him no effort to *love* the Joneses when to speak about them disparagingly was suicidal. Inextricably committed to the prickly postulates of a state-controlled etiquette, peasants were forbidden to quarrel with each other; "if this is disobeyed," a fifteenth-century edict proclaimed, "both sides will be put to death, without inquiry into right and wrong."[146] Cultivating a smile was as vital as cultivating one's acres.

Still and all, the subsistence level of a five-hundred-bushel farmer was high above that in the 250-, 100- and 50-bushel categories. A hundred-bushel farmer's house had no floor mats, a matter less of aesthetics than ascetics for in winter the wooden floor of a Japanese house feels as cold as a frozen pond to the touch of the naked foot, and only old men were privileged to wear socks. An even more draconic prohibition concerned parasols. The stoicism that makes Japanese take earthquakes, tidal waves and

252

typhoons in their stride, deserts them in the heat of summer. They crave coolness and shade more than other people do; too much basking in the glory of their ancestral sun goddess seems to have caused them a bad case of allergy. To do without a parasol is not only disastrous to a woman's complexion—be she only a maid—but downright humiliating. In Japan, even beasts enjoy protection from the sun; the lone goat at pasture, tethered to a large umbrella, is a common sight.

That contented misfit, the ten-bushel farmer, was, as might be expected, the very exponent of Japanese savoir vivre. Facing a lifetime of soup-eating without ever smelling a roast, he turned his attention to soups and became a master in their preparation. (Today as in the past, it is customary for a dinner guest to comment on the excel-

lence of soup next to that of the rice.) He would never want to drink rice-wine from anything but miniature cups—not as the diagnosticians of the inner mind would have it, because small things symbolize to him the lost pleasures of infancy, but because he was not allowed to own large cups. And his wife, forbidden to wear any footwear but bamboo-thonged sandals—that is, wooden soles with a peg for the toes to grip instead of cotton thongs—would insist that such a lowly object be fashioned with consummate skill and an eye to beauty. Today most of these objects that attest to the ingenuity and artistry of the Japanese people have been superseded by the wares of the five-and-ten; the place to look for them is in museums.

Obviously such contentment with the essentials of life (as understood in the Old Japan) cannot be imposed on a nation by a five-year plan; it takes centuries to cultivate a liking, if not for poverty itself, at least for its attributes. Envy had to be stamped out, temptation removed, communication with the outer world prohibited. Change in every form had to be abolished, inventiveness discouraged, duties and rights—or the absence of rights—perpetuated. The pursuit of happiness, as defined by our founding fa-

bamboo syringe for spraying plants, beater, and rolling pin.

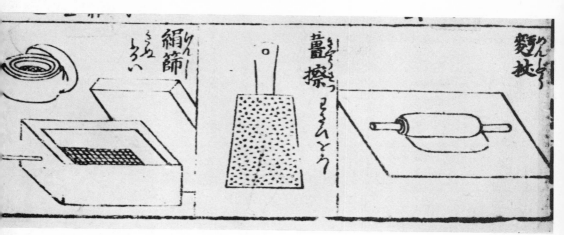

thers or today's advertising agents, was unknown to them. "The idea that the pursuit of happiness is a serious goal of life," wrote Ruth Benedict, "is to them an amazing and immoral doctrine. Happiness is a relaxation in which one indulges when one can, but to dignify it as something by which the State and family should be judged is quite unthinkable."[147]

In no other country was a man so familiar with his duties and, what is more, so eager to discharge them. "The payment of taxes," observed a student of land tenure, "did not seem to be regarded as a burden but as a loyal duty in which they took pride. The time of the annual payment, instead of being an occasion of sorrow and irritation, was more like a fair."[148] But there also were times of crises. During the Tokugawa Era—the two and a half centuries that preceded Westernization—more than a thousand peasant rebellions took place. Still, the uprisings were ineffective in loosening the bonds of loyalty and duty that gripped the peasants. Protests, if any, were always carried out with the tact and ceremoniousness characteristic of all their actions. "They would march," tells Herrymon Maurer (*Collision of East and West*), "to the daimyo [the feudal lord]

255

Warlord seated on a dais. At right, his helmet with neck-guard.
From a seven-volume guidebook to Kii Peninsula, 1809.

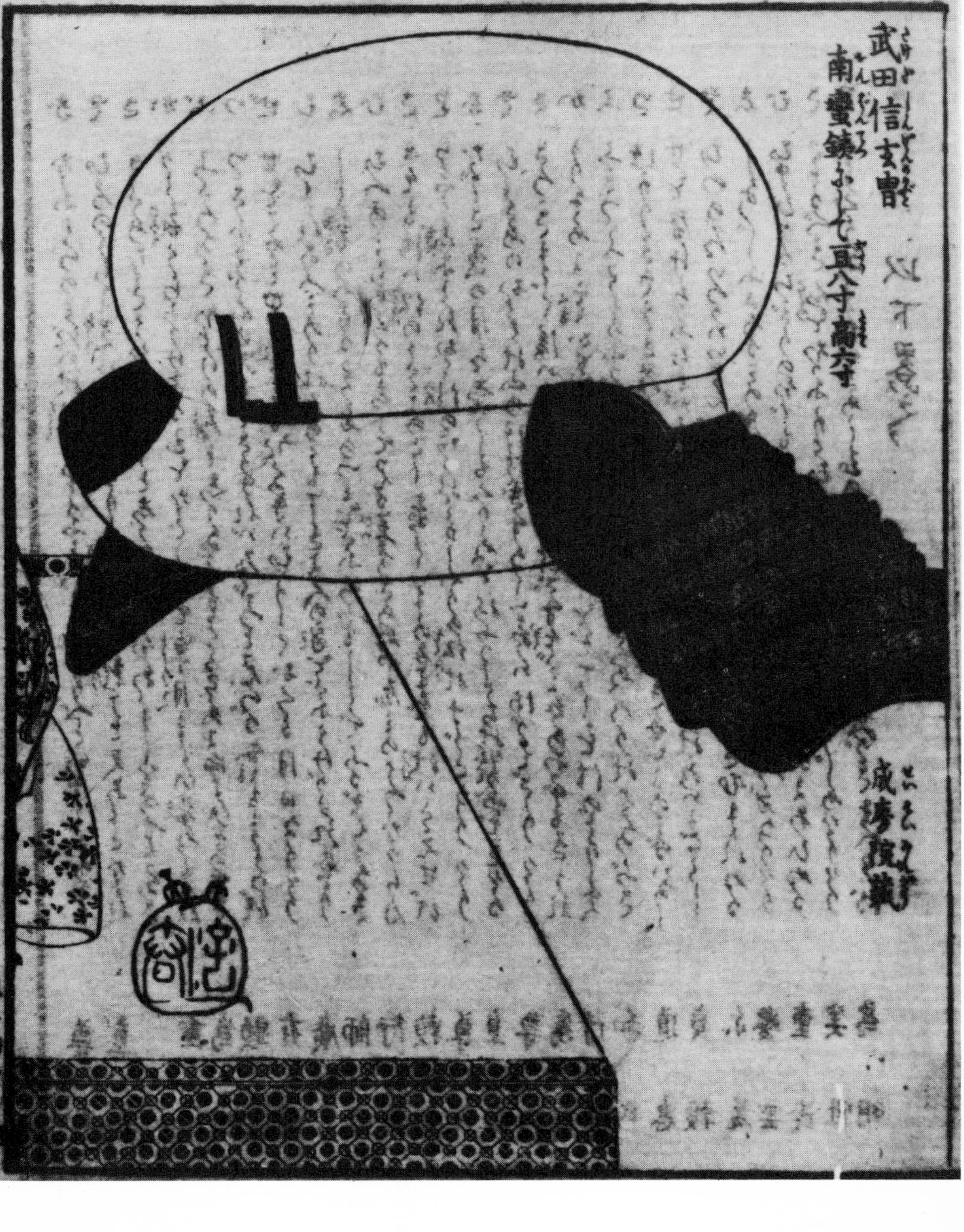
武田信玄冑
南蠻鉄ふせ 巨八寸高六寸
成瀬隼人蔵

or even the shogun with petitions; the leaders would be punished for their crossing of hierarchical lines by such deaths as boiling in oil, but the petition would be read, and in the Tokugawa Shogunate about half the petitions were judged in favor of the peasants."[149] The justice meted out was untarnished by sentimentality.

Whatever the burden of Japanese farmers in the feudal past, their houses are not at all the miserable shacks one would expect them to be—quite the contrary. Compared to *our* farmhouses, they are nothing short of magnificent, both technically and aesthetically. They have none of the architectural prissiness common to Japanese villas and tea-houses. Exploring their inner recesses, one peers at a cyclopic carpentry unknown in the Western world. The thickly thatched roof, resembling in color and texture a vast fur coat, soars from near the ground several stories high. Yet for all their majesty and charm, rural houses are not on

Peasant women from the Northern Provinces, masked to preserve their white skin.

the lists of attractions prepared for foreign tourists. The *Official Guide* ignores them. One has to hark back to Chamberlain's antiquated *Handbook* to find them mentioned at all.

The tallest of farmhouses stand in the Shirakawa Valley, some eighty miles north of Nagoya. The valley, being conveniently remote, was settled in the twelfth century by fugitives from one of the civil wars. "Peculiar customs obtain in certain villages," writes Chamberlain; "the power of the head of the family is here despotic. Moreover, only the heir (generally the eldest son) is allowed to marry. The other sons form semi-secret *liaisons,* the offspring of which are adopted either by the paternal or maternal family head, and, being considered inferior, are not mourned for when they die. Whole families live under one patriarchal roof,—brothers, sisters, uncles, aunts, nephews, nieces, grandchildren, cousins of various degrees; and the houses are correspondingly large, mostly three-storied. A division in separate rooms is seldom attempted."[150]

The houses still stand, looking as good as new, but their inhabitants have dwindled away. Modern technology has come to the valley with a string of dams built by an American construction company. With luck, some of the farmers were able to sell their houses, saving them from drowning in a modern Flood. For such is the nature and perfection of Japanese carpentry that a house built in the traditional manner without nails or bolts can be taken apart and put together again as easily as the works of a watch. Centuries before we even thought of standardization, prefabrication and mobility as architectural possibilities, the Japanese applied them to their houses as a matter of course. From economical measures these developed to aesthetic norms. To enforce compliance of poor and rich in all matters of building, the authorities issued to the artisans pre-

Household utensils.

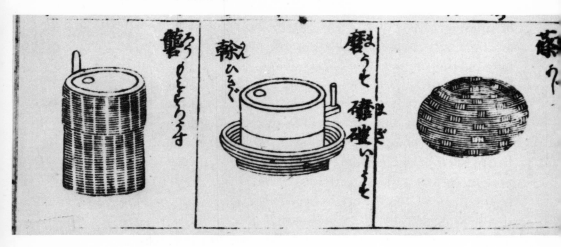

cise specifications which in time became the alpha and omega of their art.

It took a long time for the world to acknowledge the unself-conscious beauty of Japanese utilitarian things. By then, however, Japanese taste had veered from haiku to comics, from teahouses to pinball parlors. Goaded on by foreigners, the Japanese made some feeble efforts to rekindle their talents and ancient skills but the results were no more convincing than the new crop of feudal castles. Today's prevailing taste is bad taste. Occasionally it is disarming, thanks to a melancholy touch, but mostly it errupts with a withering force, like bad breath.

Lafcadio Hearn, the tireless explainer of Japanese taste, was not quite the sentimentalist his unsympathetic critics make him appear. Among his writings one finds some long-term prognostications that are as provocative today as they must have seemed in his time. "Perhaps," he wrote, "our civilization has girdled the earth only to force the study of our arts of destruction and our arts of industrial competition upon races much more inclined to use them against us than for us . . ."[151] Hearn was not so much thinking of imminent wars (although after the departure of Perry, armaments had become the paramount issue of the Japanese nation) as of the chances of biological survival which he recognized in the capacity of self-adaption to the environment "and not in the mere capacity to adapt ourselves to factitious environments of our invention, or to the abnormal influences of our own manufacture . . ."[152]

"Just as we have exterminated feebler races by merely *overliving* them," he argued, "by monopolizing and absorbing, almost without conscious effort, everything necessary to their happiness,—so may we ourselves be exterminated at last by races capable of *underliving* us, of monopolizing all our necessities; races more patient, more self-denying, more fertile, and much less expensive for nature to support. These would doubtless inherit our wisdom, adopt our more useful inventions, continue the best of our industries,— perhaps even perpetuate what is most worthy to endure in our sciences and our arts. But they would scarcely regret our disappearance any more than we ourselves regret the extinction of the dinotherium or the ichthyosaurus."[153]

"Testing Her Future," a 1760 print of odd format by Toyonobu, of a woman leaping from the thirty-foot-high platform of the Kiyomizu Temple in Kyoto.

"It became the custom for young women to test the fate that marriage had in store for them by jumping from this height, believing that if they landed without mishap, their happiness was assured." (Quoted from the Catalog of the Clarence Buckingham Collection, Chicago Institute of Fine Arts.) The enlightened modern Japanese consults one or several of the country's 200,000 fortune-tellers that function as marriage counselors, tipsters, and psychiatrists.

Forbidden Directions

Japanese streets have no names, even in Tokyo where ten million people live in unaggressive togetherness. This means that Japan has no Pine Streets, First Streets, or Fifth Avenues. Streets are anonymous. Foreigners never tire of denouncing what they consider the absurdity of this state of affairs, and the local English-language newspapers, which cater to their prejudices by printing their exacerbated letters, occasionally chime in with a half-hearted editorial. The *Japan Times* does not quite succeed in dissimulating enjoyment over their discomfiture: "That the streets in Japan except a relative few have no names is one of the phenomena which amaze the visitor from abroad."[154] Visitors from abroad whose interests exceed the repertoire of accredited tourist attractions and prefer to strike out on their own, are forever in a fix. How, they ask, is one supposed to find one's way in a town? How do the Japanese get about? For some unfathomable reason travel books make no mention of the problem. The thousand-page *Official Guide* to Japan, for example, has nothing to say on the subject of Japanese streets. Either it does not allow for the possibility of unchaperoned foreigners roaming Japanese towns, or the scholarly men who compiled the book are not aware that streets do have names in other countries.

It also happens that houses have no consecutive numbers in Japan. Numbered they are but in an altogether different manner from ours. The first house built in a district gets number one; the next, which may be half a mile distant from the first, gets number two. Hence a high number does not imply that a house is situated on a long boulevard, it merely means that the district is heavily built up. Besides, the numeration is of no consequence since it does not appear on the buildings; house numbers show up in documents only. This is called the *banchi* system.

"*Banchi*," volunteered the *Japan Times* in an expository article, "are numbers of *lots* on which houses stand, and often hundreds of houses in a big city bear one and the same number . . . A number as part of an address is of little use to anyone attempting to find it unless he happens to be highly familiar with the particular area."[155] Like many another traveler, I never found anyone in any Japanese town who was highly familiar with any particular neighborhood. Not even a deliveryman or a postal clerk. "It is a long time," admitted the *Japan Times,* "before a mailman comes to have a fair grasp of who lives in an area he is assigned to."[156] Whatever the advantages of the *banchi* system, it was *not* devised to throw bill-collectors off the scent. Neither is it a stratagem evolved by fugitives from the law, although a respectable citizen of Tokyo once told me that he avoided being drafted in the last war by occasionally changing his residence. Since a Japanese knows no other system, *banchi* does not seem odd to him.

Streets have no names, houses no numbers. The numbers on this map
refer to city blocks, not to houses, and are in no progressive order.
Besides, they repeat; number one appears nine times, number two,
fourteen times in this small area. A page from a contemporary street
map of Tokyo.

Things are not helped by the fact that Japanese towns are singularly devoid of those spires, towers, and domes that impart a characteristic silhouette to Occidental cities. The great number of modern buildings that dot Japanese towns nowhere achieve so much as an illusion of architectural urbaneness. Kyoto, seen from one of the nearby hills, presents only a panorama of several hundred smokestacks.

Whereas Kyoto was spared the horrors of bombing, Tokyo met with almost total destruction. Patched and rebuilt in a summary way, it still shows scars from years of fire raids—long stretches of no-man's-land, dumps, derelict temple grounds, and abandoned cemeteries. Only the television towers of recent date furnish signposts of a sort. If the discovery of an address is difficult in broad daylight, it appears hopeless in the dark. After nightfall, a Japanese town reverts to type and becomes the village it was in feudal times. Except for amusement centers and eating districts, gloom is the keynote of the nocturnal cityscape. Since street lighting has not much of a tradition in Japan, most streets are dark and deserted. Street lamps are still looked upon as an extravagance by people whose grandparents used to carry paper lanterns when venturing out after dark. Yet the danger of losing one's way on an evening stroll is a small inconvenience compared to the predicament of a dinner guest who cannot find his host's house.

It happens all the time. Among Japanese it is customary to fetch a guest by hired car. Americans who make it a point not to do as the Japanese do when in Japan prefer to fall back on their pioneering spirit. Instead of a limousine and a chauffeur, the hostess sends a homemade map of her neighborhood. The usefulness of the map depends on the ability of the mapmaker to pick out recognizable features from the weak physiognomy of the dilapidated cityscape. But since most Japanese cities are remarkably short of landmarks, most maps are as enigmatic as the clues to buried treasures on a desert island; the hunt for an address holds the promise of adventure.

The ethnopsychologist bent on exploring the mysterious East could not choose a better start than a brush with the *banchi* system. In order to sustain an optimistic mood in the dark of the night, in inclement weather, he will do well not to consult his watch. Regardless of distance the rule of thumb is to allow about an hour for tracking down an address—if address one can call it.

The search begins by engaging a taxicab, and nearly bogs down right there, for a Japanese cabdriver is not supposed to find his way alone. He expects to be steered like a carriage horse. In fact he looks at the pursuit of a town address as less a professional assignment than a game of chance. Withal, cabdrivers, especially those of Tokyo, are a sporting tribe. Some get deeply engrossed in the most hopeless cases, and what they lack in orientation, they make up in perseverance. It never occurs to them that their fare may be short of time, not to mention cash.

Presented with an invitational map, a driver usually makes a good show of his desire to test its usefulness and rushes off in the general direction of the goal. He soon comes to a full stop because most dwellings are situated in tortuous alleys, too narrow to admit even the smallest of cabs. Part of the scouting, therefore, has to be done on foot. Lacking specific directions, the driver inches on, picking up bits of advice from storekeepers and artisans working late hours. Barring some preposterous chance, this gets him nowhere.

The passenger who feels an urge to do his share of spadework telephones his host from some street shop, presents his apologies, and asks instructions for the driver. Alas,

267

Western logic mixes badly with Oriental intuition. The more the people who join in the search, the less they seem able to shed light on the whereabouts of the objective, which, like a will-o'-the-wisp, recedes into the night.

A people that cultivates self-mystification to such an extent would have perished had it not had recourse to superior powers. A cabdriver usually knows when the game is up and, without further ado, pulls up at the nearest police-box. Besides housing the records of all the residents in its area, it is the permanent home of a deus ex machina and his aides.

The city of Tokyo has 1239 police-boxes, strategically placed at important street crossings and near stations of the many electric lines that carry the bulk of the city traffic. They are, however, more in the nature of a gazebo than a conning tower, for in Japan street traffic is not of much concern to a policeman. Only at such crossroads of the nation as the Ginza (which is a district rather than a street) is the ritual of traffic-directing observed, and even there it is clearly done for show rather than necessity, three or four men trying to do the job of one, competing with each other as well as with the traffic lights. Elsewhere traffic swirls free-style; motorists follow their impulse rather than rules. No spoilsports, policemen leave motorists and pedestrians largely to their own devices, preferring to stay in their boxes—a snug confinement at a safe distance from the bustle of life that affords them an essentially philosophical view. Their field of vision may be not much wider than that of a Paris concierge immured in her lodge, yet, like her, they seem to have second sight. Their chief function is to put stray cabs on the right path.

Japanese policemen are not only superlatively polite, they gallantly bear the brunt of questions. They will listen with unfeigned interest to your driver's recital of erratic wanderings and, after a short council, will send him on to another police-box, allegedly somewhat nearer your host's home. Several police-boxes later, the drawback of this procedure becomes apparent. Japanese speech having a rhythm all of its own, verbal exchanges are a good deal more protracted than ours. Ideally there is no time limit for a conversation. Longwindedness being the mark of a gentleman, any attempt to be concise would be regarded as disrespectful. Prime Minister Kishi was once severely censored for delivering too short a speech at the Diet. Its shortness was an insult, the newspapers claimed. They did not say whether the speech was good or bad. Kishi had simply been short, meaning rude.

I do not know that anyone has seriously tried to estimate the symbiotic relationship between the *banchi* system and the police force; whether the function of the latter is to perpetuate the mystery of the former, or, whether the system assures the latter their daily bread. At any rate, provided you are not the frenzied type you will eventually reach your destination. The danger that the police might let you down never arises because their failure would reflect not so much on themselves as on the *banchi* system. As it is, I spent some of the most pleasant evenings in the pursuit of an address. I have come to like Japanese cabdrivers and the secrecy that surrounds a Japanese house. Some chases have had their dull moments but all repaid my persistence. When the goal is in sight, gloom changes into glee, anguish into blissfulness. With the crazy plot unraveled, the hideout correctly identified and the best route to it (which is not necessarily the shortest one) mapped out, excitement grips policemen and driver alike. The scene ends with self-congratulatory chatter and the entire cast taking innumerable deep bows. The most exultant member of the police may jump into the cab personally to conduct the triumphant finale.

Americans, not recognizing that Japan is out of bounds for Western trains of thought, play a mirthless parlor game on how to remedy the *banchi* system. It is not an absorbing game since the answers are known beforehand. In fact, there isn't a problem involved that a bright child could not solve. The Japanese, familiar with the arguments foreigners are likely to offer, are annoyed by their misplaced concern; such disputes only strengthen their belief that the intelligence of Westerners is overrated. How can foreigners hope to grasp the tenets of Oriental philosophy if they stumble over such trivia as the *banchi* system! Will they never get it into their heads that Japanese *like* their houses dark, their words obscure, their ambiguity of speech matched by circumlocution in space, their garden paths crooked, their house entrances hidden! There is no reason on earth for advertising one's whereabouts by easily identifiable streets! Even a city of ten million makes for a cozy place as long as it is innocent of street names and house numbers.

Some charitable Japanese willing to argue about the *banchi* system are apt to say that its abolition would be a hopeless enterprise. The main obstacle seems to be an uncanny Japanese talent for building nests in the cracks and crannies of towns which are formless to begin with. And there the argument rests. It is no use to remind them that theirs are not the only labyrinthine cities in the world. Indeed, the city layout has nothing to do with the plight of postal authorities and land registrars. Kyoto's street plan is as tidy as mid-Manhattan's—streets run in gridiron fashion, city blocks conform to a unit. Yet, like every other Japanese town, Kyoto, too, has its *banchi* system. To find an answer to this puzzle, one has to go back a thousand years.

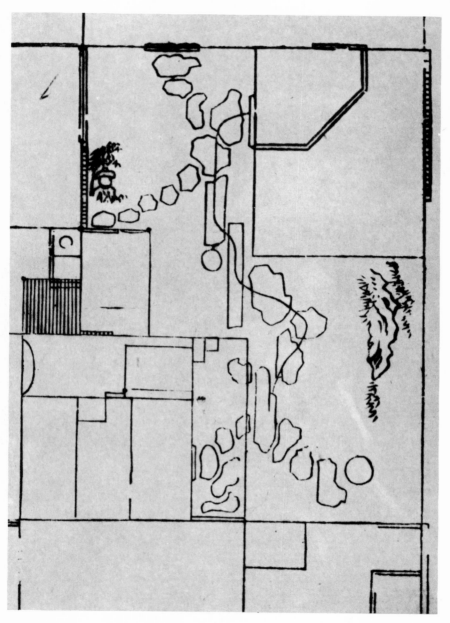

Whether or not conditioned by Fate, detours seem desirable. No Japanese garden path is straight. Its stepping stones are laid out according to esoteric rules, making a walk an aesthetic adventure.

Detail of a Kyoto map, 1864. Color woodcut.

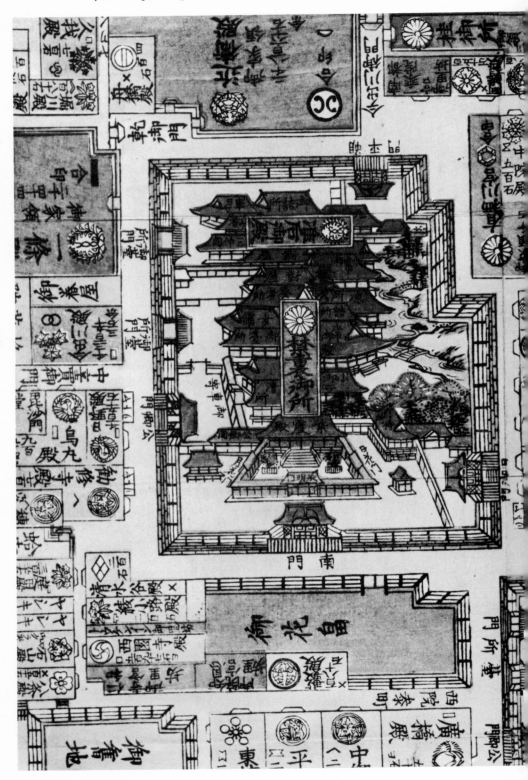

At center of page, the forbidden palace of the emperor.

Below, houses of lords and scholars, distinguished by their crests.

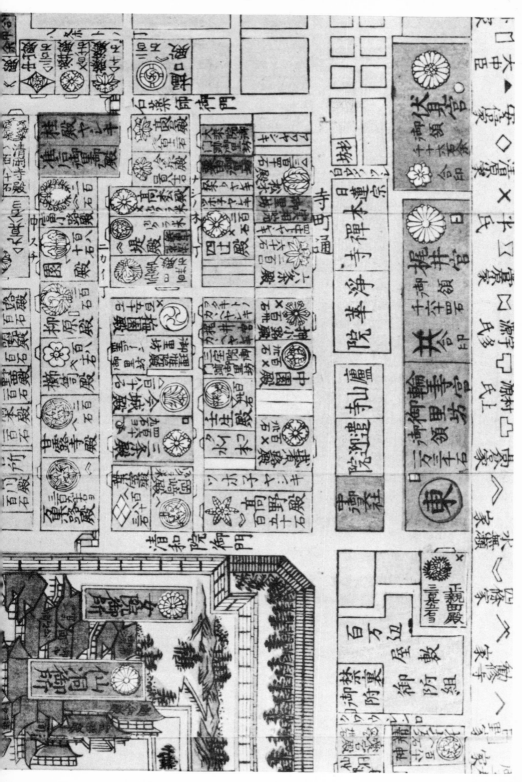

Above, palace for retired emperors.

The Japanese of old, much like the ancient Greeks, lived in a time when the gods still walked the earth; when religion was not a weekend treat but the leaven for the dough of life; when people stood in fear of deities and demons, and the foretelling of disaster was part of a day's work. Life's path was strewn with the booby traps of fate. Among the more trying handicaps was a temporary immobility inflicted by divine constellations, and when the forecast augured badly, even a short walk was out of the question. Travel posed formidable logistic problems and called for consultation of a sort of supernatural road map. "We stopped for the night, since the capital lay in an unlucky direction," notes a tenth-century noblewoman in her diary. "What direction is forbidden today?" asks her husband, much as he might say, What shall I wear today?[157]

In a note on this esoteric blindman's buff, Edward Seidensticker tells of the taboos inflicted by the movements of the gods. "Thus Taihakujin or Hitohimeguri moved to a different one of the eight directions every day, and it was forbidden to advance in the direction where he happened to be in residence (two days out of every ten were free, however, since he spent one day in the sky and one in the earth after completing a tour of the compass). Tenichijin or Nakami stayed five or six days at one point, and his direction became taboo depending on the year of one's birth."[158]

A nobleman of the time did not necessarily have much faith in conciliating fortune, and may have used superstition as a convenient pretext for shirking irksome duties. He probably expended considerable ingenuity in improvising detours, and one cannot help thinking that these complications held as much fascination for him as his elegant pastimes. To this day the Japanese have a way of calling off an excursion, canceling an appointment, or simply ig-

274

noring it without bothering to give a reason. Free as they are on the whole from individual caprice, one wonders whether they are still in the grip of the old taboos.

When that mighty conqueror with the corncob pipe descended from the sky and set out to rehabilitate the nation that had erred, it looked as if the twilight of the Japanese gods had come. American soldiers groping their way through miles of rubble which faintly denoted the former existence of hundreds of thousands of homes carpentered along the lines of horoscopes, were blissfully unaware of forbidden directions and the *banchi* system. Committed to a faceless capital, the Occupation authorities lost no time in correcting a centuries-old neglect: they baptized Tokyo's streets. Or rather they extricated from the ruins a network —tangle is perhaps a better word—of recognizable thoroughfares and marked them with conspicuous street signs (in English and at intersections only). Although thousands of lesser, equally populous paths remained anonymous, the good work cannot have but gladdened the godfathers' hearts. The soldiery, homesick as they were, must have felt a resurgence of pain when coming upon street signs with such nostalgic names as First Street or Avenue A.

Alas, the scheme stopped short of numbering the houses. Everything considered, this was probably just as well since the American authorities had no intention of taking over the burden of postal deliveries. Some of the street signs, a little battered by now and patinous from smog, are still in place, and the observant tourist sometimes notes with bewilderment that Seventeenth Street intersects Thirtieth Street, or that Fifteenth Street intersects itself.

The latest edition of an official Tokyo map, running to more than two hundred pages, nowhere mentions the abortive American street plan. Ask a cabdriver to take you to Yoyogi Street and he will sadly shake his head. To him

275

Yoyogi is a district, not a street. He has heard foreigners ask for it before, but he has long decided not to have anything to do with the American scheme. Tokyotes take pride in not knowing what the street signs stand for. A noted Japanese religious philosopher I once heard talking about his favorite subject—the inability of foreigners to understand Japanese mentality—adduced American street baptisms as an example of misplaced proselytism and giggled himself sick in the course of his lecture.

No doubt the street signs are bound to disappear with the last American soldier. Maybe some collector of cultural curiosa with a philosophical turn of mind will save a few from the scrap heap as silent mementos of the unresolvable conflict between East and West. Maybe, too, some inordinately inquisitive researcher will want to know why General MacArthur in seven years of residence never left the precincts of Tokyo. If ever there was a case of forbidden directions to end all speculations on the power of evil spirits in Japan, it seems to be his.[159]

Text references

1. *Manners and Customs of the Japanese. Japan and the Japanese in the 19th century. From recent Dutch Travels, especially the Narrative of von Siebold, etc.,* 1852, p. 14.
2. *Narrative of the Expedition of an American squadron to the China Seas and Japan, under the command of Commodore M. C. Perry,* 1952, p. 97.
3. *The Complete Journal of Townsend Harris.* Introduction and notes by Mario Cosenza, 1930, p. 433.
4. *Japan Fulbright Letter,* vol. VII, no. 3, Dec. 10, 1958, p. 4.
5. Kunio Yanagida, *Japanese Manners and Customs in the Meiji Era,* 1957, p. 155.
6. Ichiro Kawasaki, *The Japanese Are Like That,* 1955, p. 89.
7. Tetsuro Yoshida, *Japanische Architektur,* 1952, p. 179.
8. *Japan, The Official Guide,* 1954, p. 20.
9. Philip J. Terry, *Terry's Guide to the Japanese Empire,* 1927, p. xxxiv.
10. B. H. Chamberlain and W. B. Mason, *A Handbook for Travellers in Japan,* 1907, p. 6.
11. *Japan Fulbright Letter,* vol. VII, no. 4, Jan. 9, 1959, p. 4.
12. B. H. Chamberlain and W. B. Mason, *A Handbook* etc., p. 15.
13. *Japan, The Official Guide,* 1954, p. 36.
14. Kunio Yanagida, *Japanese Manners* etc., p. 27.
15. Ibid., p. 10.

16. Keizo Shibusawa, *Japanese Life and Culture in the Meiji Era*, 1958, p. 71.
17. Mary R. Beard, *The Force of Women in Japanese History*, 1953, p. 98.
18. Kenichi Kawakatsu, *Kimono*, 1954, pp. 42 ff.
19. Ibid., p. 45.
20. *Some Unpublished Letters of Townsend Harris.* Edited by Shio Sakanishi, 1941. Unnumbered.
21. Anna d'A., *A Lady's Visit to Manilla and Japan*, 1863, p. 204.
22. Charles Peter Thunberg, *Travels in Europe, Africa and Asia*, 1796, vol. III, p. 267.
23. *Narrative of the Expedition* etc., p. 220.
24. F. Brinkley, *Japan,* 1902, vol. II, p. 91.
25. Yukichi Fukuzawa, *Autobiography,* 1934, p. 135.
26. George Alexander Lensen, *Russia's Japan Expedition of 1852 to 1855,* 1955, p. 15.
27. *Japan, The Official Guide,* p. 249.
28. Basil Hall Chamberlain, *Things Japanese,* 1905, p. 2.
29. B. H. Chamberlain and W. B. Mason, *A Handbook* etc., p. 11.
30. *Japan, The Official Guide,* p. 11.
31. Douglas G. Haring, *Personal Character and Cultural Milieu,* 1956, p. 409.
32. John F. Embree, *Suye Mura,* 1946, p. 65.
33. F. Brinkley, *Japan,* vol. II, p. 82.
34. Ibid., p. 164.
35. Engelbertus Kaempfer, *The History of Japan,* 1727, p. 442.
36. *Manners and Customs of the Japanese* etc., p. 51.
37. Ibid., p. 51.
38. *The Complete Journal* etc., p. 355.
39. *Paper* by Comm. M. C. Perry, read before the American Geographical and Statistical Society, March 6, 1856.
40. *The Complete Journal* etc., p. 491.
41. Ibid., p. 482.
42. *Japanese Popular Culture.* Edited by Hidetoshi Kato, 1959, p. 206.
43. *Japanese Etiquette.* The World Fellowship Committee of the Y.W.C.A. Tokyo, 1955, p. 5.
44. Ibid., p. 7.
45. José Ortega y Gasset, *Man and People,* 1957, p. 197.

46. Ki Kimura, *Japanese Literature; Manners and Customs in the Meiji-Taisho Era,* 1957, p. 249.
47. Ibid., p. 98.
48. Inazo Nitobe, *Lectures on Japan,* 1936, p. 131.
49. Ibid., p. 131.
50. Lafcadio Hearn, *Glimpses of Unfamiliar Japan,* 1894, vol. II, p. 345.
51. Ki Kimura, *Japanese Literature* etc., p. 247.
52. John W. Bennett, Herbert Passin, Robert .K. McKnight, *In Search of Identity,* 1958, p. 234.
53. Ibid., p. 142.
54. R. P. Dore, *Land Reform in Japan,* 1959, p. 413.
55. *Japanese Etiquette,* p. 152.
56. J. W. Bennett, *etc., In Search of Identity,* p. 167.
57. D. J. Enright, *The World of Dew, Aspects of Living Japan,* 1955, p. 136.
58. *Japan, The Official Guide,* p. 56.
59. Ki Kimura, *Japanese Literature* etc., p. 260.
60. John F. Embree, *The Japanese Nation. A Social Survey,* 1945, p. 233.
61. Inazo Nitobe, *Bushido, the Soul of Japan,* 1899, p. 27.
62. Ki Kimura, *Japanese Literature* etc., p. 260.
63. *Japan, Its Land, People and Culture.* Compiled by the Japanese National Commission for UNESCO, 1958, p. 960.
64. Ibid., p. 960.
65. Ibid., p. 947.
66. J. E. de Becker, *The Nightless City,* 1896, p. 161.
67. Mock Joya, *Things Japanese,* 1958, p. 665.
68. Ibid., p. 665.
69. *Japan* etc., Jap. Nat. Com. for UNESCO, p. 947.
70. *Narrative of the Expedition* etc., p. 219.
71. *With Perry in Japan: The Diary of Edward Yorke McCauly,* p. 68.
72. Edward Seidensticker's adaption of "In Praise of Shadows" by Junichiro Tanizaki, *Japan Quarterly,* October–November 1954, p. 46.
73. Yoshida Kenko, "Essays in Idleness" (1340), in *Anthology of Japanese Literature.* Edited by Donald Keene, 1955, p. 238.
74. Arnoldus Montanus, *Atlas Japanennsis,* 1670, p. 64.
75. F. Brinkley, *Japan,* vol. IV, p. 22.
76. *Japan, The Official Guide,* p. 25.
77. Elizabeth Gray Vining, *Window for the Crown Prince,* 1952, p. 110.
78. *Narrative of the Expedition* etc., p. 157.

79. *Japanese Etiquette,* p. 17.
80. Ibid., p. 18.
81. Junichiro Tanizaki, *The Key,* 1961, p. 29.
82. Eleanor Cowles Gellhorn, *McKay's Guide to the Far East,* 1953, p. 55.
83. Anna d'A., *A Lady's Visit* etc., p. 208.
84. *With Perry in Japan* etc., p. 108.
85. *The Complete Journal* etc., p. 259.
86. Ruth Benedict, *The Chrysanthemum and the Sword,* 1946, p. 178.
87. Santha Rama Rau, *East of Home,* 1950, p. 27.
88. Santha Rama Rau, *This is India,* 1953, p. 19.
89. B. H. Chamberlain and W. B. Mason, *A Handbook* etc., p. 187.
90. John F. Embree, *Suye Mura,* p. 93.
91. John R. Black, *Young Japan,* 1883, vol. I, p. 115.
92. Ibid., p. 62.
93. *Japan, The Official Guide,* p. 222.
94. "Mabuchi River Tragedy," the *Japan Times,* July 30, 1959.
95. Lily Abegg, *The Mind of Asia,* 1951, p. 286.
96. *Japan, The Official Guide,* p. 852.
97. Engelbertus Kaempfer, *The History of Japan,* p. 95.
98. Lafcadio Hearn, *Japan, an Attempt at Interpretation,* 1929, p. 14.
99. Inazo Nitobe, *Bushido, the Soul of Japan,* p. 107.
100. Okakura-Yoshisaburo, *The Life and Thought of Japan,* 1913, p. 3.
101. Sumié Seo Mishima, *The Broader Way,* 1953, p. 114.
102. *Japanese Popular Culture.* Edited by Hidetoshi Kato, 1951, p. 31.
103. Kazuo Kuroda, "The Cult of the Sun Goddess," the *Japan Times,* March 21, 1959.
104. Inazo Nitobe, *Bushido, the Soul of Japan,* p. 11.
105. *Narrative of the Expedition* etc., p. 219.
106. Luis Frois, S.J., *Tratado em que se contem . . . algumas contradições e differenças de custumes antre a gente de Europa e esta provincia de Japão* (1585), 1955, p. 250.
107. Robert S. Schwantes, *Japanese and Americans,* 1955, p. 189.
108. Ichiro Kawasaki, *The Japanese Are Like That,* p. 75.
109. Yukichi Fukuzawa, *Autobiography,* p. 135.
110. *The Complete Journal* etc., p. 422.
111. Edward S. Morse, *Japan Day by Day,* 1917, vol. I, p. 440.
112. Philip J. Terry, *Terry's Guide* etc., p. xviv.
113. Ibid., p. xxxv.

114. Awaji-no-Kami Muragaki, *The First Japanese Embassy to the U.S.A.,* 1920, p. 62.
115. *With Perry in Japan* etc., p. 81.
116. *Narrative of the Expedition* etc., p. 208.
117. Katharine Sansom, *Living in Tokyo,* 1937, p. 21.
118. *Japanese Etiquette,* p. xi.
119. Ibid., p. 50.
120. Ibid., p. 51.
121. Ibid., p. 55.
122. *Narrative of the Expedition* etc., p. 138.
123. Ichiro Kawasaki, *The Japanese Are Like That,* p. 130.
124. Luis Frois, S.J., *Tratado* etc., p. 252.
125. Keizo Shibusawa, *Japanese Life* etc., p. 66.
126. Ibid., p. 65.
127. *Some Unpublished Letters of Townsend Harris.* Edited by Shio Sakanishi, 1941. Letter of October 22, 1856. Unnumbered.
128. Ibid., letter of July 16, 1858.
129. Chitoshi Yanaga, *Japan since Perry,* 1949, p. 94.
130. B. H. Chamberlain and W. B. Mason, *A Handbook* etc., p. 10.
131. Yukichi Fukuzawa, *Autobiography,* p. 121.
132. D. J. Enright, *The World of Dew* etc., p. 139.
133. Kunio Yanagida, *Japanese Manners* etc., p. 147.
134. Mock Joya, *Things Japanese,* p. 45.
135. Ruth Benedict, *The Chrysanthemum* etc., p. 180.
136. *Manners and Customs of the Japanese* etc., p. 86.
137. Charles Peter Thunberg, *Travels* etc., vol. III, p. 107.
138. B. H. Chamberlain and W. B. Mason, *A Handbook* etc., p. 327.
139. Elizabeth Gray Vining, *Window for the Crown Prince,* p. 203.
140. Charles Darwin, *The Descent of Man,* 1871, p. 327.
141. *Japan, The Official Guide,* p. 15.
142. Jiro Osaragi, *Homecoming,* 1954, p. 211.
143. *The Complete Journal* etc., p. 360.
144. Ibid., p. 428.
145. Ibid., p. 360.
146. Herrymon Maurer, *Collision of East and West,* 1951, p. 87.
147. Ruth Benedict, *The Chrysanthemum* etc., p. 192.
148. "Notes on Land Tenure and Local Institutions in Old Japan." Edited from the posthumous papers of Dr. D. B. Simmons. By John H.

Wigmore. *Transactions of the Asiatic Society of Japan,* 1891, vol. XIX, p. 59.

149. Herrymon Maurer, *Collision* etc., p. 88.
150. B. H. Chamberlain and W. B. Mason, A *Handbook* etc., p. 275.
151. Lafcadio Hearn, *Out of the East,* 1895, p. 238.
152. Ibid., p. 240.
153. Ibid., p. 242.
154. "Numbers of Houses," the *Japan Times,* July 14, 1959.
155. Ibid.
156. Ibid.
157. *The Kagero Nikki.* Translated by Edward Seidensticker, p. 131.
158. Ibid., p. 15.
159. During the Korean War, General MacArthur left Japan a few times to visit Korea. Still, his travels in Japan amounted to no more than the trips between Tokyo Center and the airport.